What To Do With A Million Dollars

by Thomas W. Neely, Jr.

Woodcock Publishing
Williamstown, Massachusetts USA

What To Do With A Million Dollars

 For information, address Woodcock Publishing, Eph's Alley, P.O. Box 209, Williamstown, MA 01267.

Library of Congress Catalog Card Number: 96-61377

ISBN 0-9655032-1-6

Book design: Zane C. Lumelsky
Copy editor: Alan H. Green

Published by Woodcock Publishing
Printed in the United States of America

First Edition: January 1997

To Elaine, Matt and Bree

Contents

Introduction

What To Do With A Million Dollars will cover everything except how to spend it. Each chapter tackles a separate question. It's better if the reader tries to sort out his or her purposes ahead of time. What will you wish to do with your life that in any way involves this money?

A very large number of millionaires want most that money not change their lives. This may mean driving that American sedan, living in an ordinary neighborhood, earning indifferent income, never paying retail, practicing any number of comfortable economies. Research has confirmed how common these sentiments are.

Others have long hoped to notch up their level of existence. A million dollars can aid enormously in doing so, but it doesn't permit real lavishness. Several million might, at least for a time.

Lots of people with money today want to help society, the environment, culture, medicine, their alma mater or community. In the past organized religion ranked first in the thoughts of many. More often than we might imagine it still does.

Seeing after family members is tricky. Unstintingly helping one's parent or child in need often seems an open and shut matter. But paying a relative's tuition, investing in a relative's business, "gifting" large sums, helping someone out of a tight spot all can raise matters that turn into disputes. Questions of fairness, motives and judgment pop up out of nowhere. Never just assume your family will be different. And never assume just because it's "your money" that relatives will fear to advise you.

But we're talking about you. What would you choose? If you haven't already determined what you want to accomplish, I find the most effective way is to write down your personal policy. It should be a statement that tries to clarify any goals you have for the money. Take care to cover both the short and long term. Some people can sum everything up in two sentences. Usually a paragraph is enough. Even if you're not used to writing things out it's by far the best way of establishing precedence for financial objectives. Do it now. At least get started. If doing this proves impossible for you, finding out won't take long.

Being responsible for lots of money needn't be stabilizing or destabilizing, as such. It is a fact that inheriting big money out of the blue can grow into a burden. Most of us, though, just have to find the level of action vs. detachment that lets markets work while steering us away from persistent errors.

Few qualities in life are as unevenly distributed as maturity. Years of experience, though, have taught me that "maturity" is the best way to say what one needs to handle sizable sums well.

A lot of good money-handling skills and attitudes may look counterintuitive the first time we meet them. When told "The biggest risk is to do nothing," for instance, we ask how could something like that ever be true. Warren Buffett observed that it's not the learning, it's the unlearning.

Financially immature people are either wasters or

savers. But neither is plain right or plain wrong. The fully developed person is a mixture. Similarly, beginners may be risk takers or loss-averse. Experiments supposedly prove that people would twice as much prefer not to lose a dollar than to gain one.

As we pile up experience (and experience pileups), we learn hard truths. Money is symbolic. Just having an account involves trust and compromise. People may want autonomy, but they have deep fears. Fear of the financial future prevails today. Recognizing and admitting these fears lessens their control over our behavior.

We may notice, as we rise toward maturity, that investors overreact to quick changes. They under react to slow ones. Knowing this gives us emotional ballast. An overzealous, systematic budget manager can deteriorate into a tightwad. Maturity gives a perspective that prevents this type of distortion. You don't want to be a serial spender either.

Mature managers of their own destiny always follow through. They don't neglect the final step, whether it's choosing an adviser, funding a trust, or changing a residency. Mature people distrust the myth of sufficiency. There's never enough money for this myth to become real. More money itself rarely results in lowering uncertainty beyond a near point. Mature people simply take measures today to finance outlays in the future. You become what you pretend to be, Kurt Vonnegut warned. So we have to be careful about how we shape our ultimate psychological makeup.

It's almost a necessity to keep a list or log, even a

mental list, of your aims. Automatic course corrections in financial or investment behavior follow.

Similarly, the affluent shouldn't just use money to smother conflicts that should be openly resolved. Insulation and isolation from life itself are well-known hazards to young inheritors of huge amounts. Seasoned people must remain in the stream of life to benefit most from their own good fortune.

Serious money, like great beauty, draws the attention of many persons we'd as soon not deal with. It can be hard, but it's an absolute requirement to balance a defense against predators with underlying good will toward the world at large. Constant suspicion of all others goes hand in hand with the kind of obsession that prevents the enjoyment of having money.

A mark of maturity is to look at conflicting evidence extra hard, like a scientist. Seeking other views is central. When someone (spouse, counsel, friend) is found to have serious investing/financial skills, mature people know to hand over control and not to second guess.

Once you've wrestled to Earth your personal philosophy for the money, a big question hangs overhead. How do we make sure we don't foul up the savings and investment part? That's what much of *Million Dollars* concerns. Before dipping into details, though, we must think about investment objectives. Don't worry; there are only a few. I'll list them first: liquidity (accessibility), safety, income, growth of income, growth itself, tax advantages and speculation.

Seldom do any two investors have the same mix of

objectives. Safety always proves important to a great many investors. Liquidity may or may not. Even if your cash flow is good, keeping six months' living expenses in cash or the equivalent never hurts. Income I find the easiest objective to figure. You either need and want it from your investments or not. Maybe now, maybe later. Even the amount isn't hard to calculate.

Growth means having the aggregate value of your holdings go up. Growth, which can cut into income, is often a requisite to protect the real value of financial assets. *Real* means adjusted for inflation. A million dollars now will sooner not later be worth only $500,000 in today's money. With a successful growth program you can have $2 million instead. Thus you preserve real capital. For many that's the paramount objective. Look for a deeper discussion of growth in the part of "Hanging on to It" in Chapter Two that deals with preservation of capital (see page 29). Growth is the main focus of Chapter Four.

Growth of income is different. It implies that the amount of revenue produced by investments rises consistently. The point? To preserve buying power. Inflation erodes buying power as we are often forced to notice. If income from your holdings is a key objective now or eventually, it's a good idea to arrange for income increases that at least run neck-and-neck with inflation.

Tax advantages are a magnet to crowds at the seven-figure level. Far too many people, however, worry only about income tax. In fact it's estate or even gift taxes that can really demolish accumulated capital. To curtail income tax, we sometimes need to receive tax-exempt income at certain times when we just don't want more income of any kind. One type of municipal bond, by the way, called zero-coupon, automatically reinvests tax free to maturity day. No income goes out. The bond just grows in value.

Congress tinkers with tax-policy compulsively. Capital gains rates rise and fall. Income brackets creep back and forth. Deductibles and depreciation schedules are never safe. Just keep in mind that a representative or senator's first responsibility is re-election. Doling out or even the mere exploration of doling out tax advantages keeps campaign funds coming in. Same with imposing tax disadvantages. This, as long as we're a democracy, cannot change. Even a huge change, such as moving to a flat or perhaps a consumption tax, would be lucky to survive more than one administration. Remember 1986?

The other income-tax-favored technique is deferral. With growth stocks, for example, companies reinvest earnings to develop new things to sell or to uncover new markets or the like. They therefore don't pay dividends. This can be good because dividends are "after tax" for the company and pretax for you. Twice taxed, in other words. With growth holdings you pay tax only on profits when you sell. Often that's many, many years later.

Annuities, IRAs, Keoghs 401(K)s and all the many "qualified" pension plans have as their chief benefit the ability to delay income or capital gains taxes for any type of security they contain.

Estate and gift taxes are much worse at the millionaire

level than most minds can fathom. Fortunately the means to reduce them are quite comprehensible if too often ignored. Be advised that federal and state tax planners will make this area even more of a danger zone.

If the Amount is:

(A) More Than	(B) But Not More Than	Tax on (A)	Tax Rate on Excess of A
$ 0	$ 10,000	$ 0	18%
10,000	20,000	1,800	20
20,000	40,000	3,800	22
40,000	60,000	8,200	24
60,000	80,000	13,000	26
80,000	100,000	18,200	28
100,000	150,000	23,800	30
150,000	250,000	38,800	32
250,000	500,000	70,800	34
500,000	750,000	155,800	37
750,000	1,000,000	248,300	39
1,000,000	1,250,000	345,800	41
1,250,000	1,500,000	448,300	43
1,500,000	2,000,000	555,800	45
2,000,000	2,500,000	780,800	49
2,500,000	3,000,000	1,025,800	53
3,000,000	10,000,000	1,290,800	55
10,000,000	21,040,000	5,140,800	60
Over 21,040,000	–	11,764,800	55

Unified Credit: $192,800 (Equivalent Exemption: $600,000)

Unified Federal Estate and Gift Tax Rates
Figure 1

Speculation is the only type of investing that some people know. They call their stockbroker and ask, "What's hot?" For sensible people, speculation should not tie up more than 5 percent of financial assets. Period. A majority of market participants never knowingly speculate.

The foregoing sketch of objectives leads us to investor timetables. But first let's look at the variety of ways we think and feel about investing.

The more years an investment plan can remain in effect the more predictable its relative results. We know from academic studies how much various asset formulas have tended to produce over periods of such-and-such duration. What the reader needs is to decide or at least guess when money will be spent in the future. Medical expenses are usually the great unknown. Most of us, though, can put on a piece of paper the approximate dates when unusual outlays can be expected.

Objectives should dovetail into a timetable so that our investment plans have to be changed as little as possible. Returns on investments are far superior when we can allocate or label funds "do not disturb" for a good long while. The short term volatility present in certain investments tends to vaporize over periods of time. This cuts the size and nature of their risks.

If the number of years an investment can continue are important, equally so is the stage of life of the investor at the time the investment occurs. A 40-year-old hasn't much in common with a 65- year-old as to typical objectives. Objectives change as we move out along our own time lines. Our personal economic policies and practices reflect the way we're living.

So far so good. But what if you're asking just how will I, an investment lay person, be able to set my assets up in a way that lets them meet my targets? How can I balance income now with future income needs, for example? How can I stop being too safe? Or too unsafe?

One thing for sure is that you earmark certain assets to attain certain results. We will look at how to do this from several angles. Chapters Three and Four take each objective one at a time. The various ways to satisfy each come next. Although most millionaires properly seek professional advice, *What To Do With A Million Dollars* arms the reader so that his or her needs are always served ahead of those of the adviser.

By now we see that taking care of goals after they're established is 90 percent of *What To Do*. Concern for certain objectives overlays different chapters. "Where to keep it," Chapter One, occupies itself with safety. "Hanging on to it" relates to three objectives: safety, growth and tax-advantages. "Taking what you want and need" tells us what will deliver income, liquidity, growth of income, tax advantages or any combination of these aims.

Chapter Four, "How to make it grow," concerns appreciation and the relatively exotic question of speculation. The last chapters cover charity and inheritance planning, topics which stand to the side of most investment questions.

To keep your financial records and information up to date and always at hand, use technology that combines investing and banking. Personal visits to branch banks are trending down rapidly. Phones, ATMs and computers take their place.

Do business only where they appreciate you and don't deal with you as a number. The concept is "high tech-high touch." When technology does the routine work, it's more important that personal encounters be caring, respectful and efficient. When you sit down and talk over your finances, you need to be treated like an important person.

An account must be the type that keeps track of stocks, bonds and any mutual funds or unit trusts. It collects interest and dividends. You want good news and bad news brought to you. CDs and bonds can be called or prerefunded unexpectedly. Stocks go through mergers, splits, tenders and so forth. The right account monitors and reports such activity. It has convenient unlimited checking and low-interest borrowing, all spelled out on one comprehensive statement. The blizzard of mail in your box subsides.

Chapter One

Where to Keep It

A million dollars is a financial asset unless an unusually large part remains, say, in real estate or perhaps art or another "tangible." Financial assets whether we like it or not should be housed in finance corporations. This means investment companies, banks, brokerage houses or hybrid boutiques that serve as reliable custodians. Not one of these as a type proves inherently superior. A good bank is better than a bad broker, and so's the reverse.

Allow me to size up the pros and cons of available choices. I'll start with brokerage houses, the band of the spectrum where I work. But I'll be as fair as possible. Each option has real virtues.

Investment Companies

Brokerage houses to me mean companies like A. G. Edwards or Alex Brown that have a large number of individual or "retail" clients. They survive business and economic cycles by giving most clients what they need, or at least what they want. Largely the representatives, called brokers, counselors, salespeople, consultants, account executives, managers, or even planners earn their living by recommending the purchase or sale of sundry financial assets.

Although you may eventually spend time with service persons more routinely than with a representative, it's he or she you discuss investing with. These sessions should be extremely educational to the inexperienced investor.

Much of the time the broker resembles a teacher. For experienced investors new developments in securities, taxes and the economy ought to be something the broker can place in perspective.

The broker must listen carefully to anything the client or potential client says about money, risk, personal history or hopes and fears. The client thus makes known how much and what kind of counseling is proper.

Bound by rules to act on the client's behalf the broker should go by guidelines of "suitability." To that end the legal and regulatory injunction is "Know thy customer." That the broker also knows securities cold is assumed, not always correctly.

The common-sense investor often frames some questions that for reasons of tact go unasked. One is, "How much do these people really know?" The other is "Why would a commission salesperson put my interests ahead of the broker's?"

How much investment advisers know is usually quite a lot. But unless the adviser has a narrow speciality, dependence on the firm's recommendations remains a real life necessity. Some parts of any firm's advice turn out better than others. This is where experience and perhaps instinct let the broker pick and choose more wisely for the client. At all times in the securities universe certain asset categories outperform. A broker succeeds if the way he or she allots securities in his clients' portfolios does better than the averages in down markets and doesn't underperform by much in up markets. It's even better if performance consistently exceeds averages, but for the client to do quite well that kind of superiority isn't required. Expecting it is unrealistic no matter how much advisers know.

When serious amounts of money need investing, and you are uncertain of the broker's savvy, ask the broker to put the recommendations and their rationale in writing. The quality of the prose doesn't matter. What you're looking for is knowledge, earned authority, a vision or strategy and an underlying plan. Most important of all is the connection between what you want – your objectives – and what the proposed securities are expected to deliver.

With a written proposal in hand you can seek others' opinions. This brings up the matter of exactly whose advice do you seek in the brokerage house world anyway. A referral from a trusted person is a great way to start. Another is an interview with managers of firms. You don't usually want a manager, in my opinion, as your broker. Managers should be too busy anyway. You want a recommendation based on who would do the best job, not who needs the business or whom the manager owes a favor. When the manager suggests someone, ask why. Ask about the person's qualifications, experience and similar accounts.

Don't automatically reject less experienced persons. Sometimes they work hardest and care most. Fresh out of training, they may know about up-to-date developments of which veterans could be unsure. In general, though, as we know, there usually isn't a good substitute for experience in any kind of adviser, unless you yourself happen already to be well-schooled in the subject.

There are times when a broker won't prepare proposals until assets are transferred to his firm. This needn't be a bad sign. You can transfer assets out just as easily as you can transfer them in, should you not care for the course of action recommended. Obviously no authority to "reposition" your assets is delegated until you have great confidence in either the broker or the investment proposal or both. In some cases investors give brokers written authority to control their accounts. This we call *discretion.* It relieves people who are bored silly by securities of feeling responsible for decisions. But taking part in every step at the early phase of a client/adviser relationship remains the best education for the millionaire. Education equals protection.

The item of self-protection brings up the question of whether clients come first or commissions. Broker training and education stress doing the right thing for the client. Except in gallows humor I have rarely heard securities salespeople admit they were putting their own interests ahead of their clients. I've worked for three distinctly different firms. We all believe that a good reputation leads to the referrals that help brokers prosper. We ask, do surgeons recommend surgery just because they're paid to operate. No answer to this question deals with the whole range of professional conduct.

And yet – and yet. Even with the best intentions at times it's almost unavoidable for a great many otherwise decent brokers to look at what's good for them as well as the client. Sensible clients of course never object to their brokers' earning money. A sort of invisible running tab, however, should inform their consenting to portfolio moves that may not be demanded by circumstances. To use the surgery comparison again, do only what has to be done. Measure twice and cut once.

Up to now I've skirted the societal puzzle of poor professionalism in finance. How great a problem is it? When you measure the gross amount of misconduct and stupidity against the trillions of dollars invested perhaps the percentage is quite tiny. I'll grant that I don't see evidence that it's not. But the outrageousness of taking advantage of those who've bared their financial souls makes me burn. What is the solution?

Regulators already police the industry from within and without. Still, investors must remain vigilant, almost detectivelike if they don't think that everything's just right. I don't have a magic charm for detecting trouble. However, there's a method that almost always works.

Ask the adviser about something troublesome, be it poor performance, high fees, lack of suitability or whatever. Listen carefully to learn if there is in fact an adequate explanation. The keystone of this approach to problems is as follows: Ask exactly how your troublesome matter fits into the entire conduct of the relationship. You want the broker to restate the premises you've agreed on and to explain how the problem is part of that whole. If the broker acted in bad faith it would take a verbal Houdini to cover it up this way. If the question doesn't resolve itself then and there, ask either the manager or a trusted authority whether you're off-base in your suspicions. No innocent people will resent an honest inquiry. The relationship that survives will be stronger I assure you with the broker or adviser knowing you really care about policy and details. If the relationship perishes, nothing will be lost except time. And the investigation itself has real educational value.

To discover whether a broker was disciplined by industry, state or federal regulators use the 800 number of the National Association of Securities Dealers, 269-9999. The NASD will also report any criminal convictions. And to find out at the state level who handles requests of this type, ask the North American Securities Administration Association: (202)-737-0900.

A *fin-de-siècle* phenomenon likely to persist is unauthorized taping of conversations. Reading accounts of disputes and trials, I'm surprised how often the subject comes up. You won't have to worry if you discipline anything you say to a possible adversary.

Brokerage companies do not levy custodian fees. All accounts at A.G. Edwards, for example, carry $2 million in insurance and premium accounts $25 million. More is available. Other similar companies take similar measures.

Fees, commissions and markups at brokerage houses hinge to a good degree on the relative commonplaceness or unusualness of a transaction. All costs tend to shrink relatively as transaction size increases. As a very rough rule of thumb 2 percent or less of a fair-sized retail stock transaction can be expected, whereas 3/8 percent to 5/8 percent or slightly more may be a normal bond markup. Large United States Treasuries at some firms are bargains, costing only 1/10 percent or less commissions or markups. Money markets at brokerage firms are for client convenience. Their yields therefore run a little higher than at institutions where these short-term mutual funds are an important profit center.

Grounded in transactions, brokerage houses don't charge a lot of other fees. A total asset account with checks, gold cards, insurance and interpretive statements will cost $75 to $100 a year. Sometimes there's a $50 annual charge for open accounts that are totally inactive. I personally would not keep an account that charged a fee just for the purpose of keeping it open. For IRAs there are small fees.

Money managers are popular with six- or seven-figure account owners. Managers make investment decisions with the securities residing at a brokerage firm. Expect to pay 1 percent more or less of asset value a year for this service. As an interjection, plain old brokers who are authorized to make and carry out buy and sell decisions without the client's OK can't charge extra for it. Although the client may feel more comfortable with the broker as the manager, only extremely rarely can brokers display the years of audited performance records that are money managers' trademark.

Two developments started to catch on in the 1990s. "Wrap fees" are inclusive charges of perhaps 3 percent or less, diminishing with larger accounts. They cover any costs of transactions, great or small, that the manager makes. Included as well are the manager's fees to run the portfolio. It's advantageous per se to have an upper limit fixed on transaction costs. This is one way to accomplish that.

In my experience, though, investors assess all managers by rapport first, performance second, and fees, which are a drag on performance, last.

The other potentially revolutionary mutation is "performance based" fees. Managers who offer this deviation from the norm make up a tiny minority today. But the idea shows great public appeal.

What kind of role does financial planning play in brokerage house accounts? Although financial planning, like marriage counseling, is an ultimately unregulated profession, responsible groups and associations give the practice a semblance of structure. Some planners charge hourly fees or job fees to work out solutions for clients. Others more or less live by the sales charges of financial products they recommend as part of their plans. Don't be surprised if a planner takes it both ways: fees plus sales charges. You're on solid ground, though, if you object to paying two ways.

It would take an unusual planner to have the time, energy and intellect also to be an investment adviser. The way planners often handle this is by selling or recommending mutual funds or limited partnerships whose goals align with client objectives. "Growth" funds, "income" funds, "tax-exempt" funds are examples. The only problem appears to be that the difficulty of choosing good funds isn't too different from choosing good stocks. Overconfidence in mutual funds plagues financial planners, banks, the press and the inexperienced.

Banks

Bank trust departments house a large part of well-off families' money. Some accounts simply hold assets safely for the disposition of owners or the appointed controllers of the assets. This isn't usually a highly favored alternative from the bank's point of view. Fees are low and the banks don't want to be mistakenly identified as endorsing the accounts' investment practices in case things don't work out.

A more common type of account, often referred to as an "agency" account or an investment management account, shouldn't differ in form wholly from an ordinary stock brokerage account. Investment officers of the bank's trust department may obtain the client's permission before buying and selling securities. Fees add up to very large amounts. At least they're large enough that they should be explained ahead of time.

The type of account that most people mean when they say agency is a discretionary arrangement where the bank's investment officers make and execute portfolio decisions. No trust agreement or document is drawn up, and the arrangement can be dissolved in a matter of days.

One rung up in complexity is a living trust account at a bank. Without our going into it too deeply this early, living trusts are revocable and thus don't offer all the advantages or disadvantages of other trusts. Although the bank is named as trustee or successor, another trustee can be appointed, in effect terminating the relationship.

Most trust accounts are irrevocable in the sense that going to court would be required to upset the arrangement. Lawyers draw up the agreements in ways that should meet trust clients' long-term needs. The point is clear that utmost caution early in the game could have a good outcome over the decades.

The department deducts fees as a percentage of the whole, usually around 1 percent. In addition there's a basic cost of several thousand dollars a years. All bank trust departments have continued to increase fees, it appears to me. In many instances fees are charged simply to collect income from dividends and interest. If both fees are working together the bite on your capital can add up fast. Always ask for a fee schedule. Should charges seem out of line, visit two-or-three comparable trust departments. Client alertness on fees instructs the staff not to assume you'll take excessive markups or mysterious debits lying down. It never hurts to be perceived as a little prickly. Actively managing $1 million trust account can run to $15,000 a year. Elsewhere, it can be done for a fifth of that.

What about performance? Is it good enough to make up for high fees? Trust account performance at times at certain banks appears overstated. A typical professional comment on a trust department's "record" is, "I don't see why everyone doesn't have an account there if they're that good." It's obvious to us that they're not. Another observation I've heard is that, "The accounts at Bank X all seem to perform well except in those instances of which I have firsthand knowledge." Be wary, in other words. No close scrutiny or regulatory monitoring can be depended on to restrain these performance claims. A simple statement such as "Our top stocks have averaged X return" may mean only that their best performing stocks do that well. *Not* the stocks most clients own the most of.

Among people who toil in the investment vineyard trust departments sometimes have the reputation of being a little sleepy. In an overpaid money universe, personnel there are not overpaid. They're anonymous, not publicized. There's a suspicion, perhaps exaggerated, that mediocre, even submediocre accomplishments go unpenalized. Of course under performance isn't always rewarded.

"Better sleepy than sleazy," I'm sure trust officers could reply. By and large they've retained their reputations for probity. Even if the bank around them collapses from risky loans and investments, assets in the trust department are never thrown into settlements. They remain separate and safe.

Trust department statements can serve as paragons of obfuscation. At more than one bank, and this is hard to believe, senior officials have admitted they have no idea what certain important items mean. The assumption is that all these details look just too complicated and serious for clients to worry about. Behind that kind of veil, we gradually learn, lie all kinds of surprising fees and charges.

One advantage that trust departments have in certain instances is that they can act as trustees for family and other trusts. Don't mix up these two concepts of trust, by the way. The usual legal concept of a trust has the trustee holding title to something for the benefit of another.

Although the trustee may be a bank, there is no presumption that it need be. Often it's not, in my experience.

The advantage of having a bank as trustee especially for long-lived trusts is that it should endure as an institution without interruption. As this is written, however, the banking sector is undergoing unprecedented consolidation. Trust departments, once consolidated, may move to points on the map hours away. It's not as if Morgan Guaranty can't have accounts, and probably does, in Anchorage. It's just that for many people money is such an important, intimate matter that they prefer contact of some kind in a nearby community. The tendency nationally is for banks to slice and dice trust operations through this period of cannibalization and shrinkage.

Even if a bank disappears the trusteeship continues at a successor institution bound by the same trust agreement. Though sensitive subtleties may be lost, the heart of the agreement abides. At a later chapter we'll delve into various pluses and minuses of picking certain types of trustees. And remember that just as some banks can process securities trades, it's not too unusual for a brokerage house to own a trust company for trust account purposes. Actually, it's commonplace now.

An alternative that seems superior on several counts is the small insured non-bank professional trustee and executor. They're smarter, better, cheaper and faster. Year-end taxes and other paperwork are folded in if appropriate and desired. Revenue collection and bill paying are useful features available to clients who have more interesting distractions. These firms not only play a fiduciary role. They know clients inside out and can provide good judgment in my experience.

Discount Firms

Perhaps responding to the thicket of full-price alternatives, people often explore discounters. Although I work for a full-service brokerage company, people ask for my honest opinion about discounters. I couldn't endorse the concept more if I tried. We who grew up in the '50s can remember those so called "fair trade" laws that stopped retailers of much merchandise from discounting. How infuriating even then. And who wants to establish a full-fledged medical relationship just to check out a rash, or to "retain" a law firm before having the wording on a simple buy-sell agreement checked out? Who wants to pay $2,000 for a cashmere coat at Polo on 72nd Street only to see it in Freeport for $299?

Discounting is great, in other words. Is it for you? Almost certainly not. Why not? Relying on discounters you have to become your own expert. And if you have time to become a millionaire securities market expert, you must be living at least two lives.

Discount firms as you probably know don't counsel customers as to buys and sells. So far as I'm aware they do an adequate job transacting stock business for less than half the cost of full-service firms. People who know exactly what they're doing – relatively few – and who don't benefit from bouncing ideas off a broker can well use a discounter.

The analogy of the travel agent applies to "products"

such as limited partnerships, most mutual funds and all unit trusts. They cost the same at a discounter, so you may as well get a broker's advice from a full-service firm. And it cannot happen that a discounter could ever bc as helpful with a portfolio of tax-exempt bonds and Treasury notes as brokers with that specialty. That's just one example.

Trading your own portfolio by computer is another advantage to the skilled private investor. For most people, however, it just makes it easier to commit investment gaffes.

The tragicomic irony of discount firms is that those who know least about securities may be most drawn to discounters. No cushion exists between them and panic when this year's or next year's crisis arrives. Meanwhile the pros or semipros who have much less need of a full-service broker use them anyway. Often their trades are so large that they automatically get discount rates no matter which type of firm does the business.

Years ago there were only a dozen-or-so securities assets an investor could purchase. Now these are over 50, and many of them trap the unwary even if that's hardly the purpose of the security's design. The person with other interests doesn't want to spend hours with his or her nose buried in the business press for self-protection. Depending on discounters reminds me of cutting your own hair. Bypass it unless you know exactly what you're doing.

One persistent enemy of sound investing is panic. There always was and there always will be something alarming in the United States or world economy. Both the government and the press benefit from stirring this pot:

You turn to them for solutions, surrendering power. A non-discounter adviser benefits from guiding you through periods when others are panicking. He or she earns respect, leading to more business. The only way discounters benefit is through commissions. Even if they gave advice – they don't – one might fear it was tainted, adding to panic.

Family Office

Family shop or family office are quaint terms for the private, often exclusive firms that concentrate on handling several facets of privileged persons' financial affairs. Yes, they manage investments. But they may not stick to securities. Tax limitation programs, household budgeting and bill paying, charitable gifting, estate planning, dealing with the IRS and so forth are their kinds of services and activities. Fees seem high. But look at what you get: freedom from financial headaches. That's worth a fortune to lots of millionaires.

Drawbacks of family offices, or real private banks, besides the expense of their services, include high minimum account size. Don't be surprised when it's several million dollars. Then there's the inevitable possibility that you might be viewed as a small fish. I haven't run into this much, but senior clients don't always relish having 23- year-old Ms. Pointdexter make her bones managing their elsewhere respected account.

More on the positive side, and this isn't the place to explore it, these elite boutiques can connect clients with private non-public investments. Real estate is an obvious example. So is venture capital. Petroleum exploration or development has turned out well for many private investors. Besides this, the range of fiduciary services surrounding public and private asset selection is usually complete.

As when you consider setting up a relationship with any company, be a little skeptical of performance figures family shops may show. There should be evidence of an outside audit before you swallow them.

Asset Safety

The safety of financial assets isn't quite the delicate matter it may have been for Grandfather. I'm referring to safety in the sense of protection from physical damage and protection from disappearance or loss. Bad investments, whose value shrinks or vanishes, receive attention later on. It's a separate matter.

Some people prefer to keep their stock, bond and other certificates at home or the office. A good safe should hold these documents. Complete, accurate lists should stay with the lawyer, broker or in a safe-deposit box. Securities are replaceable but large non-refundable bonding costs can result.

Safe deposit boxes are favorites of fans of physical possession. I know of only one case where investors think something happened to a security in one of these containers. That was the case of a bearer (negotiable) bond believed to be missing. It's not anything, given all the measures taken, to worry about.

People have their own reasons for holding their securities themselves. Among them you hear privacy, portability and plain enjoyment from doing the associated paperwork: clipping coupons, checking off dividends, counting and listing the certificates. Behind the scenes measures are underway to eliminate physical certificates in the next few years, you will find. Government bonds have turned the "book entry only" corner. Copying the federal government, most municipal, or tax-exempt issuers have now followed suit.

When you sell securities kept in safe-deposit boxes or at home, you must use registered mail if sending them to your broker. Maintaining an accurate list of certificate numbers is another task. A safe-deposit box incurs a maintenance charge. Retaining securities at home brings the inconvenience of locating and handling them. You risk loss through fire or theft. The three-day settlement standard has increased the "aggravation coefficient" in holding one's own stock and bonds.

If securities are "domiciled" at an investment firm, dividends and interest are collected and credited to your account. Custodial service provides an accurate and permanent record of dividends and interest, eliminating check handling, depositing and general paperwork. Interest and dividend income can be remitted to you weekly, monthly or quarterly, depending on your requirements. The amount of dividends and interest paid is recorded for tax purposes. To facilitate filing, total income credited to your account during the year shows up on your statements.

If you own bonds, at their maturity date the institution

holding them for you presents them by computer to paying agents for redemption. Proceeds go promptly into your account. Unexpected calls and redemptions trigger immediate contact between the firm and you.

You may own stock in a company which is offering additional shares through a rights offering, or in a company which offers to purchase securities you own by a tender offer. Timely notification from the firm holding your shares is a certainty. Whatever your wishes at the time, the institution follows through. And if you hold securities that must be exchanged due to a merger or other corporate development, you eliminate the need to locate, document, and mail these securities to the transfer agent. Firms forward to you all proxy material and transmit your response to them. Insurance coverage of securities in seven figures is often provided free of charge. Remember that clients with cash management accounts are protected to a total of $25 million to $150 million per customer.

* * *

Short answer: Keep all financial assets in an insured brokerage account that combines banking and investment services. Develop a trusting relationship with your customer's man or woman. If unable to do that, change advisers.

Chapter Two

Hanging on to It

Logical though it may be I'm not certain that cheating and thieving bedevil millionaires more than others. Would official crime statistics with their shortcomings prove anything? Regardless, securing assets persists as a universal concern among society's "haves." Except for illegal money transfers by computer, most of the ways criminals use to fleece people have deep historical antecedents.

Theft, Schemes and Ostentation

Theft is so commonplace that law enforcers and the courts can shock us with their offhandedness. Not that they don't care, but other "more serious" crimes occupy them even more. Depending on where you live, do take measures that are typical for the area and then some. With a videocamera, walk through your house recording valuable furniture, art and other transportables. You can have this done professionally. If your home contains antiques or designer items of high value, call an appraisal service to do a workup. Any on-premise safe had better be the best available. Otherwise use bank vaults. Insure to the point of diminishing return.

As to security systems that rely on electronics or private patrols, it's up to you. One leaves normal life behind if too much interference with routine is required. If the systems used in your neighborhood work well, though, why not? It's not yet to my taste, but affluent residents of gated communities express overall satisfaction with their choice.

Kidnapping for ransom may not be an appropriate item of discussion for the hyperimpressionable. Like fire drills, however, going over the "what-ifs" probably can't hurt the average well-off family. Consultants, like Kroll and Co., help if kidnapping looks to be a real danger. Even bodyguards aren't just for the famous.

Confidence schemes so intricate and elegant that nobody could resist them are found more often in art than life. Putting one's trust in the wrong persons is the real-life threat. Hideous indeed are those existences, granted, where all outsiders are viewed with suspicion. We must acknowledge, however, that cheating and swindling the prosperous has always consumed the energies of social desperados. At no time will this change. You play the great game now. It will stay essential that you not take financial or investment advice at face value. Your advisers should win your confidence first unless trusted associates, relatives or friends vouch for them unreservedly. Sometimes even that's not enough.

An assertiveness of manner coupled with (unprovable) claims of investment success often seems to dissolve defenses of the otherwise blasé. Perhaps it's a widespread suspicion that one has never been cut into the really great deals oneself. We remember things we could have invested in that turned out well. We forget those we avoided that failed.

Something makes us vulnerable. Sometimes it's the illusion of urgency. The "urgency" claim is of course to stop us from investigating. I might ask, "Why is it my luck to learn of this opportunity so late in the day?" Never be rushed.

Outright flimflam may be easier to spot than investment deception. In the interest of eluding tricks, keep away from proposals where you alone have to put up, or "front," the money in the deal. If there's other money in play you must see proof that this is so. Always request details in writing. Seek views of CPAs, lawyers or investment advisers. State or federal regulators can often help.

If the investment concept seems unusually complicated, keep going over it until it's comprehensible. One detail to investigate is any recourse you would have should things go wrong.

You don't have to be worth seven figures to receive requests for inappropriate loans. Too rare is the individual who consistently lends money sensibly and for lack of a better term, professionally. Except in highly informal settings, see that your lawyer draws up agreements of a sort common to banks and lending agencies. Typical loans between persons may carry an element of speculation. A 5 percent-of-assets rule as to maximum speculation should include amounts lent as well as invested. Always try to secure a private loan with collateral. Charging high interest rates if you wish is justified for the most part.

Preserving Capital

The frame of mind needed to preserve capital rests on one simple principle. This is the principle: It is far more important almost all the time for most people with money to preserve capital than it is to add to it. I'm referring to real, inflation-adjusted capital. You can relax about missing the boat or those too-good-to-be-true deals. Avoid investment decisions based on only fear, greed or excessive sentiment. It's not that hard when your overall goal is appropriate and attainable.

How you live can determine the level of risk, aggravation and solicitations you attract. Often in America the display of wealth, it has been said, isn't consonant with its possession. Think of all those long-term-leased Porsches and powerboats.

Avoiding ostentation drains tension out of your life. I'm not counseling people on style, but much of what is done with money isn't admirable. A good rule if you want something badly is to wait six months to see if your desire is still strong. Whether it's a horse, car, painting or piece of real estate you will often find your lust to possess has vanished.

How does this pertain to not being tricked out of your money? As a practical matter a lower profile, perhaps more "authentic" way of living, may not always repel swindlers over the years, but it will attract fewer of them. This is delicate territory. After all one of the points of having money is to spend it any way you want. If your way remains the flashy way, so be it. Cultivation of the quieter paths of expressing and spending wealth does bring many rewards. Not least of these rewards is keeping yourself out of the cross hairs of those who would wrongfully win your assets away.

In the spirit of common sense let me remind readers how discretionary even the fairest applications of tax law can turn out. It's kind of reverse triage. And it applies to every level from property assessments to the Internal Revenue Service. How much sense then does it make to have your way of life screaming "I have money! I spend money!" Revenuers can't help pricking up their ears.

I wanted first to cope with immediate, sometimes sinister attempts to loosen your grip on your capital. Actually, *preserving capital* as a catch phrase refers to something different. Preserving capital has to do with planned activities that keep your money's value at least even with inflation. If you had $2 million and inflation were to compound to 100 percent over a period of years (something that's happened repeatedly) your $2 million is now valued at $1 million by the standard of the period's start. To equal the original $2 million you need $4 million. Or you have not preserved your capital.

When responsible financial advisers, accountants, lawyers and some bankers discuss their frustrations a leading subject is the well-off person who thinks savings accounts preserve capital. Error! Let's say your income is 4 percent and inflation is 3 percent and taxes nick you for an additional third. In real terms you have a structural, that is, locked-in, erosion of capital.

Appreciation, or growth, is the pathway to preservation of capital in "real" terms, which we remember means adjusted for inflation. A half-million dollars in 1970 is worth a fraction of that now. A half-million dollars invested in 1970 in assets that appreciated could be worth many millions in nominal (unadjusted) and real terms today. And this without what anyone would label spectacular performance.

Ordinary Americans have widely achieved appreciation via home ownership. For a variety of intertwined reasons, real estate isn't seen as excelling during the next decades as it did in the not distant past. Still, appreciation in desirable properties can outrun the Consumer Price Index. Thus ownership of ordinary residential property for most people shouldn't be surrendered. Real estate as a class of assets can still work in many locales.

Common stocks are the vehicle of choice for growth. In what ways do growth stocks differ from other equities? Instead of paying out after-tax dividends to be taxed again as personal income, growth companies redeploy profits internally. Through research and development and seeking out and expanding new markets, these companies aim to enlarge their own value. The investor pays just one tax (when selling at a profit). But within the holding period she or he should have benefited from untaxed, thus larger, company earnings working away inside the company. When long-term capital gains taxes are low, in-pocket potential is even greater.

Whether you end up managing your own investment destiny or delegating it out, you'll benefit by familiarizing or reacquainting yourself with some equity (or "stock") market basics. Stock selection (picking winners) may seem the ticket to favorable equity investment outcome. Literally, yes. But I'm convinced by studies and personal experience to favor something called *sector selection*. A sector is one slice of the whole financial/commercial/ industrial pie. It exceeds individual stock selection in importance by an ample margin. In other words equity performance turns much more on how much is allocated to each sector than to each stock. Looking primarily at the sector has its own term: top-down. Putting stock picking first is naturally called the bottom-up approach. Let's call them investment styles.

What are these sectors? They may not be quite as easy to name as you'd think. Just the act of trying to define the big industry groups, the macrosectors, can collapse into differences of opinion. Does transportation belong under "Basic Industry" or does it have its own sector? Where do conglomerates go?

Because this exercise is not academic, there's no choice but to be pragmatic. How the sectors actually behave in the economic cycle's stages is the question, not how they should behave. Suppose that transportation, traditionally underweighted late in a bull market, is hit by merger-mania in trucking and airlines. Or oil prices dive. Maybe the formula should then be modified. Maybe not. What works is the test.

Before showing what I think is a workable division of stocks by macrosectors which embraces various industry groupings of companies, I must comment quickly on market timing. This is an extremely wide-ranging term. It refers to shifting assets among sectors as a response to economic change. We should remember that it doesn't take a genius to see that fewer cars will be bought in a recession. That gold-mining stocks don't thrive during disinflation. That people have to have medicine and food at all points in all business and economic cycles. Market timing works best if at all when it anticipates moves in the business cycle. Often we follow moves, reacting too late.

"Basic Industry" if you think about it includes chemicals, forest products and paper. Not so obvious, perhaps, are construction and one of today's active business groupings, pollution control. Count steel and aluminum too.

"Capital Spending and Technology" as a macrogroup covers whole heaps. Machinery, equipment, aerospace, electrical instruments, computer systems, software and defense electronics. It's about 18 percent of the Standard &Poor's by market value. It's controversial, by the way, but I think biotech belongs here. Behaviorally, certainly, if not abstractly.

"Consumer Cyclicals" depend on how flush the buying public is or feels it is. Retail, restaurants, leisure, automobiles, media and apparel. This many-faceted sector even brings in building materials, toys, and gambling.

"Consumer Staples," at almost 20 percent probably the heaviest weighted S&P 500 sector, includes drugs, beverages, health care, food, cosmetics, containers, soap and tobacco. You'll hear "defensive" and non-cyclical applied to this group.

"Energy" embraces not only oil but natural gas, coal and the oil service industry.

"Finance" some call "financial services." "Interest-sensitive" and "interest-rate related" are synonyms too. Banks, insurance companies, savings and loans, securities brokerages and other investment companies.

"Natural Resources" is mining and timber and such.

"Transportation" includes airlines, railroads, trucking, shipping and air freight.

"Utilities" are made up of the private electric, natural gas, water and telecommunications industries.

"Miscellaneous" is where I put advertising, real estate investment trusts, and conglomerates too diversified to fit in elsewhere.

Later we'll discuss shifting assets from some of these microsectors to others. It's called sector rotation. Conventional market counselors often affect a fatalism about investors' ability to do this. Many professionals say it's too hard to discern ahead of time which sectors should improve. They point to the fact that business and economic cycles never repeat themselves predictably. Another persistent fact of investment life remains the tendency of money managers and amateurs alike to buy into price momentum. That means getting on board those sectors that are already heated up – the bandwagon. That this is often a bad idea proves very difficult to remember for some reason. A practice of some "sector rotators," concentrating too much in too few sectors, deserves condemnation, too. Wipeouts happen this way.

Without some form of sensibly diverting assets from one area to another, we deny ourselves the use of our knowledge of the world, of our very common sense. When one part of the portfolio becomes outsized, it can be trimmed of some appreciated assets. The proceeds then put into areas found to have shrunken in value or not to have grown as much.

Let's go over this approach again. Call it static asset allocation. There is such a thing as dynamic asset allocation, but it's a jittery game played by pros with giant sums and narrow margins. All static asset allocation means is keeping your slices of pie the same relative size. If stock is 75 percent, then it stays 75 percent even when the stock market goes up or down.

If the market goes up you sell stock until it's 75 percent again. What did you do? You sold high. Should the stock market decline, you add to the slice until it's 75 percent again. You bought low, by definition. The money you took from selling stocks you then put into something that's down, ergo cheaper. To buy stocks, you take from some sector or slice that's up.

This simple technique applied once-or-twice a year works wonders toward guaranteeing that objectives are met. "Your personal financial platform" is how I term this in *Investing Without Worry* (1992).

Revising Insurance

The insurance vantage point that many affluent people grew up with needs another look. Policies are so complex that in effect we appease the insurance gods by paying off large multielement deals that often no longer fit.

A professional method to make insurance dovetail with reality is to look at every policy separately and force that policy, in effect, to justify itself. It often can't. Ask why did I buy this? Was it right? Have conditions changed? Can it be done cheaper or not at all?

Let's cover the basics of important insurance solutions to some problems that were treated differently by past generations.

Disability insurance coverage may be the prime omission among many working people's plans. To say it's essential understates things. It doesn't cost much considering the high risk of some kind of disability during a career. You're not nearly as likely to die, and you're insured for *that*, as you are to become disabled.

Probably fewer than a third of American companies make any kind of disability protection available. Frequently even those policies aren't topnotch. Two-thirds or more of your income for an indefinite period should be replaceable with adequate disability coverage.

Insurance to pay long-term care (LTC) serves much of the market *What To Do* deals with. The poor will receive free care. The awfully rich "self-insure," paying for nursing home care privately. The merely well-off among the rest of us stand about a 45 percent chance of entering a nursing home if you live to 65. Good nursing homes, surprisingly, can have discharge rates up to 50 percent. You receive care and then go home. You want to have money left over.

Today's typically encountered health condition among seniors is frailty. You need a lot of customized help. Perhaps you live for a very long time. At $50,000 to $200,000 annually, you could impoverish yourself over the years. If you voluntarily impoverish yourself ahead of time to get state support, your family may lose a certain amount of interest in you. This is a sad fact, but a fact.

Qualifying for Medicaid requires the depletion of

savings and assets. In case we forget, Medicaid is simply welfare, with a friendlier name. Medicare, incidentally, isn't much help at all. It pays less than 2 percent of all nursing home costs nationally. Yet more than half the people I meet think incorrectly that a long term nursing home stay will be financed through Medicare.

Most non-insurance industry professionals recommend picking up an LTC policy in your mid-60s. It may cost several thousand dollars a year with an inflation rider. The decision to buy the rider is a lay-up considering how even moderate inflation shrinks buying power over a decade or two.

Needless to say you can be bumped from many insurance companies' consideration if your medical status is even borderline. Once on board, though, your rates don't go up unless the whole category you're in rises.

ADL (activities of daily living) differ from skilled nursing care, which is hospital-like. Make sure a policy covers both. And home health care. And Alzheimer's. And Parkinson's. A good policy will.

As medicine changes through the next decades, your policy must be adaptable instead of exclusionary. Do the very best you can on this point. In states with strong regulatory commissions like Massachusetts, officials may simply mandate that a new or improved care technique be paid for. That safety net should grow: Ultimately improved treatments save everyone money most of the time.

Probably 4 million people already have long-term-care insurance. As states run out of tax money, more ways will be found to force people to pay for their own care with savings or insurance.

Again, in the 1990s, the best age by consensus for millionaires to buy long-term-care insurance appears to be around 65. There are advisers who suggest 55, though, when rates prove quite manageable. If you're working, incidentally, and have ordinary medical coverage, a stay in a long-term-care facility would be paid for at least as far as skilled (not custodial) care goes. The premium depends on how long a waiting period you choose before coverage takes over costs. Coverage for life costs more, of course, than coverage for three years, and so on.

In insurance today, the biggest in-your-face bargain is a large umbrella policy protecting us from personal liability. Automobile accidents jump to mind. For $200 or $300 a year, $1 million in coverage can be obtained. You may want more, but put down this book and buy at least $1 million if you don't already have it. Maybe the litigation volcano will die back one day. In the meantime, people with a million bucks are sitting ducks in liability cases. If you face decisions about medical insurance, let this focus your mind. A policy that would pay $2 million in medical bills may be worth more than everything else you've got, put together. So make sure any lifetime benefit limit is somewhere in seven figures. Drugs and outpatient care should be taken care of, not to mention all hospital and surgery costs. I suggest at least a $1,000 deductible and a co-payment of perhaps 20 percent.

As far as conventional whole life insurance goes, the operating assumption should be that you don't need it except for estate or inheritance planning purposes. Naturally, inexpensive group life at work is a justifiable good buy when you can imagine your family members getting a plump check fast should something happen. But, for the most part, your $1 million or more, and how it's handled at your death is the key concern. For many of us (I've been guilty too), not-well-thought-out purchases of large life insurance policies have substituted for more painstaking financial planning for thinking, in other words.

We'll explore life insurance solutions to inheritance questions later. In general, a policy held in a separate trust can make up for assets earmarked for an aggressive charitable-gifting program. This program in some cases can produce tax and income pluses that far outweigh the cost of insurance. The separate life insurance trust, keep in mind, removes the valuable policy from the name of someone who could otherwise have it become vulnerable to estate tax levies. You want it out of the estate and in a trust.

For the last few years, sales of second-to-die policies have moved to the front as a simple solution to steep tax problems in estates. You are probably aware that any assets owned by a spouse can be inherited free and clear by the survivor in a marriage. The problem comes if the second-to-die person leaves over $600,000 without a careful, advanced arrangement. The simple arrangement is a large policy to pay off taxes.

Another popular insurance industry product is the variable annuity. All a variable annuity amounts to is a no-load mutual fund within a tax shelter. Unlike the otherwise comparable IRA, the annuity permits contributions (non-deductible) of any amount. In Chapter Five, we'll discuss growth with tax advantages. That's where variable annuities fit in.

There are variable annuities which guarantee or insure that the amount of your investment will not shrink. And there are death benefits, too. But in essence the variable annuity is just another investment that reflects particular objectives.

Further, the old fashioned annuity, which is not an investment, has a new life. The anti-estate-planning philosophy taking modest hold among some financial planners relies on this insurance company contract. As you probably know, a certain amount of money given to the annuity company guarantees regular payments for a period of time or for life. You no longer risk outliving your money. We'll discuss the "die poor" point of view in Chapter Three. Traditional, conventional planning still points to dying rich as preferable.

The pros and cons of all sides of annuities will be discussed. Let me not miss this opportunity to stress that you trust your financial life only to the safest insurers. A.M. Best Co. rates these companies. Make sure the one you choose has an AAA rating going back well into the 1980s. Then make sure the annuity company is awarded a highest rating from another agency, such as Moody's Investors Service Inc., which is quite strict, or Standard & Poor's Corp.

The public can receive several ratings free from Moody's (212-553-0377), S & P (212-208-1527) or Duff & Phelps (312-629-3833). Weiss (800-289-9222) and

A.M. Best (900-555-BEST) charge to give out information. It's not a large fee, though. Telephone first.

Because your future is at stake, you may also ask if high risk assets are under 200 percent of total capital. High-risk assets are junk bonds, real estate loans that fail to make payments, and so on. The annuity company's total capital should add up to at least 5 percent of invested assets. Sounds low, I know, but that's the way insurance companies work.

Before we move away for now from insurance, it's almost always advisable to bunch your policies with one-or-two companies if you can. Property and casualty coverage for houses, second homes, cars, boats and the like can cost 10 percent less if all are with one insurer. The paperwork proliferation ebbs a bit too.

* * *

Short answer: Lead a prudent life. Use common stock to build capital nominally so your worth stays stable vs. inflation. Buy long-term-care insurance and, if you're working, disability as well.

Chapter Three

How to Take What You Want and Need

Income

All retirees need income, but the large majority have looked to a pension, perhaps, or Social Security or bank interest. Millionaires have to have another type of income: from investments. Sometimes, though, it's to supplement a job, business or professional earnings.

Income makes up part of "total return," the agreed-upon measurement of investment progress. The other part is growth or appreciation. During periods of acceptably low inflation, now being a good example, an annual total return of three times the inflation rate is a good target. When inflation erupts, as in the late 1970s, I wouldn't argue with a total return of perhaps twice the Consumer Price Index inflation measurement.

An early step in sophistication is to think of the capital, or principal, you've accumulated as empowered to yield a stream of income. You may hear seasoned authorities speaking of an investment "throwing off" income. All throwing off means is producing or yielding.

Once we decide to dedicate financial assets to producing income, we usually think next of safety. Safety of principal, that which is meant by credit risk, at first may appear uppermost in importance. Against that of course is the equally natural and opposite fear of missing the boat. In this chapter we'll treat several types of safety and risk. The investment professional's task is to let one type of risk offset another. Buying a bond, to cite one instance, avoids various risks of doing nothing. I'll bring up safety as we dig into how best to get all the things we want – and not just purely income – from investments.

The safest income generator on the planet remains a United States Treasury security. It's simple: They can print the money they owe. "They" are the sole economic, diplomatic and military superpower. About your only risk is market risk. This means the value of a U.S. security should fluctuate with changing interest rates, international fortunes and a dozen other things (see Appendix). But, no matter what, you will receive your income on time and get your principal handed back to you on maturity date.

Treasuries is the term for direct obligations (debt) of our national government. Notes and bonds come in prices of $1,000 and have durations of as much as 30 years or as little as next month, depending on the maturity date you pick. Importantly, states cannot collect income tax on income from Treasuries. Separation of powers, Marbury vs. Madison and all that. This ups your effective (in-pocket) return.

The very short term or "cash equivalent" Treasury is called a bill, usually a T-bill. And there are STRIPS, which grow in value rather than pay out interest.

Other triple-A bonds backed by Washington are called "Agencies." Lots exist. Let me group them by whether or not the interest they pay is taxable by states. (Remember where to find this information: Banks and investment professionals usually have to scramble to get it straight.)

Exempt from state tax are FFCB, FHLB, FICO, SLMA, REFCORP and TVA.

Not exempt is interest from FNMA, FHLMC, GNMA or PEFCO. Full names of above issuers are Federal Farm Credit Bank (FFCB), Federal Home Loan Bank (FHLB), Financing Corporation (FICO), Student Loan Marketing Association (SLMA), Tennessee Valley Authority (TVA), Federal National Mortgage Association (FNMA – "Fannie Mae"), Federal Home Loan Mortgage Corp. (FHLMC – "Freddie Mac"), Government National Mortgage Association (GNMA), and Private Export Funding Corp. (PEFCO).

A caveat is to beware the unknowing purchase of agencies, such as GNMA, that return principal either regularly or before you want it. The industry term *wasting asset* sounds the proper negative note. GNMAs can help in odd situations, but the trouble is that GNMA is repaying, and too often you're spending, little chunks of your own capital each month.

The second safest asset class is municipal bonds. Issued by states, other non-national government organizations, and not-for-profit outfits of all kinds, these bonds pay interest that is free of federal income tax. If issued within the state where you live, the bonds escape state and city tax as well.

Because tax-exempt municipals avoid the tax man, they can get away with paying lower rates. You, the buyer, still can end up with a greater spendable return, as you keep all of what you do get. Although these bonds test out as unusually safe under their own steam, you can stick to insured AAA bonds, still receive a good return, and own an item that's easy as pie to resell should you desire.

Corporate bonds that are supersafe don't really pay but a hair more than Governments (Treasuries), so what's the point? *They* can't print money. They are subject to state and city income tax. Fewer than 10 corporations win AAA ratings anyway. Those corporate bonds that are less safe pay 3 percentage points (or more) higher interest than comparable Governments, the benchmark. The line between high-yield and mere junk depends on who's defining it. Because all bonds are contracts (debentures) between the issuer and the owner, they are senior obligations that usually are paid off. Academic studies during the 1980s found that high-risk bonds more than compensated investors with higher returns. Subsequent studies, as we have come to expect them to, refuted the earlier studies.

Most of us in the field think that high-yielding bonds are best bought through mutual funds for diversity and professional management. Funds have disadvantages, but their good points outweigh the less good when buying bonds of doubtful quality. As a rule, although millionaires can afford some credit risk, millionaires don't have to take chances to squeeze out a few extra points in yield. As a rule.

A word or two on CMOs: Collateralized Mortgage Obligations are a hybrid – some would say bastard – breed of AAA bonds when sold at the consumer level, to "us," that is. A pool of mortgages is arrayed so that payments reach the investors only as a predictable monthly flow of interest for a specified period. That period can be soon or late: Estimated life dates of CMOs are available in hundreds of durations. Eventually your capital is returned, as in a bond. Unlike bonds, however, CMOs don't specify the precise date and can't usually arrange for all the original investment to come back at once.

Owing to the amount of uncertainty involved with CMOs maturing, they have to pay a point or more in extra interest. Often backed by GNMA or FNMA, they aren't exempt from state or of course federal tax. Bear in mind that for most people not knowing the precise date of maturity may matter less than receiving an extra 16.6 percent income (the difference between, say, 6 percent and 7 percent).

Besides offering income and relative safety, fixed income investments are just that: Fixed income as such does not increase to preserve buying power lost to inflation. But we're talking just about income now. "Growth of income" lies ahead.

Before leaving bonds let's consider the effect of tax change proposals. Drastic ones first. If we abandon income taxes, a tax-exempt bond should be like a raincoat in the desert: little need, hence less value. The bond would of course continue to pay the "coupon" (interest) and would return principal at maturity. States, however, would have to retain or increase their taxes, wouldn't they, to pay the higher costs of borrowing brought on by less valuable, hence higher yielding, municipal bonds. *Cui bono*? State-tax-exempt Treasuries and agencies.

The positive feature for tax-exempts is that a broader market would be available. Foreign buyers and pension plans could be tempted. Banks which once upon a time bought most "munis" would weigh in again.

What would replace today's income tax? If it were a flat tax, income would still determine the amount paid, and it should fall somewhere between 17 percent and 23 percent. The consumption or national sales tax (or its variant, the value added tax – VAT) would make income irrelevant in computing how much we pay. You pay only when you buy a good or service. Consumption taxes have the bonus of netting the underground economy. Money from drugs and other unreported activity, even babysitting, has to pass through the cash register and thus can't escape this type of tax.

Under consideration now are serious proposals that would eliminate any taxes on dividend or interest income when the flat or sales tax kicks in. Owners of financial assets, such as securities, would rejoice. Suffering, presumably, would be real estate. The reason is that mortgage deductibility could also disappear.

Ultimately, it's impossible to infer precisely how, first, these proposals will look as law; and, second, the effect they will have on investments. Too, the law of unintended consequences always takes over when taxes go through the wringer. Without question, the direct benefits to business of tax reform will at first overshadow benefits to investors. Not for long, though.

Still on the subject of income and not growth of income, let's now examine stocks after bonds. Mature companies usually pay off a large part of earnings in the form of quarterly dividends. These dividends, as I write, come from "after tax" corporate dollars. Yet we as stock owners must also pay personal tax on what's paid out. Eventually Washington will wake up and stop harmful double taxation. I believe this destructive practice exists only in the United States among major countries.

Today debt interest, either from bonds or loans, isn't taxed for corporations. The payments they make are pretax, in other words. What's the result? Because maximum return to investors remains the goal, "debt and not equity (ownership or shares)" ends up favored by companies. Not good. The economic outcome of cockeyed legislation always proves negative for at least a few. In this case, it's negative for all of us. Corporate financing strategies are distorted to duck the tax man.

The market of course adjusts to whatever "is." High-dividend stocks thus trade cheaply enough that pure income seekers buy them. Usually it's electric, water and gas utilities that pay well, as do real estate investment trusts and many natural resource and energy companies. We want high returns. Recall, nonetheless, that dividend yields 1, 2 or 3 points above those of otherwise comparable companies are often God's way of telling you the dividend will be "reduced." Also recall that, differently from bond holders, stock owners have no real *claim* on dividends. Every single dividend at every quarter must go through the board of directors' approval process. A type of equity that is senior to common stock we call *preferred.* Preferreds have no claim on a dividend either. But all preferred dividends must be paid before any common dividends. Typically, preferred shares return more than common because preferred dividends never increase. The climate of interest rates and to a lesser degree the fortunes of the issuing company determine if these fixed-income hybrids move up or down.

A clever method of obtaining high preferred dividends while not foreclosing yourself from *hopes* of appreciation is "convertibles." These preferred stocks (or bonds) can be changed into common stocks with a push button. That means they go up when their companion common stock goes up. But usually they go down less when common shares decline. Their big dividends (or interest in the case of bonds) confer "yield support." Any problems with convertibles? Just that not a whole lot of companies ever issue very many. There are enough, though.

Certificates of deposit (CDs) are fixed-income investments that come due (mature) usually in the not-too-distant future. Five years is a long time in the world of CDs. When insured by the FDIC or FSLIC, these pseudobonds are safe and often competitive. CDs originate in banks but are widely available elsewhere. In the last decade-and-a-half the chief problem with these certificates has been "reinvestment risk." The definition of that risk is you haven't locked in a good rate long enough. The last dozen years it seems that every time you "roll over" your CD, you earn a lower rate. This in a world of slowly but inexorably climbing expenses and prices. There's a penalty at the bank for cashing in a CD in advance of maturity. Therefore, it's often better to buy them at a brokerage house so that your only risk is "market risk." The definition of *market risk* is that you don't know ahead of time exactly how much the certificate will bring in the market. It could be more or less than you paid for it. Don't forget to acquire no more than about $90,000 or $95,000 in CDs from any one bank or thrift (savings and loan). That way you won't exceed, with interest, the $100,000 average limit imposed by the Federal Deposit Insurance Corp. or the Federal Savings and Loan Insurance Corp.

Annuities date back to the 1890s. They were popular contracts where a living allowance was paid to a dependent or a beneficiary. The type of annuity that belongs in a discussion of income involves the purchaser paying a premium to enjoy a guaranteed rate of interest. To receive income now, the customer chooses an "immediate annuity" that can offer lifelong income. Or a fixed number of years can be selected for payment. Arrangements to continue income for surviving spouses work out well in most instances. Choose companies with AAA ratings by two-or-more agencies going back five or 10 years at least. As I write, the yields these companies are posting aren't that impressive. Do shop around, but don't forget that we're in a period of long-term rate declines. You may not find yourself able to lock in even a mediocre rate for very long. They're not free, but inflation-adjustment riders are obtainable through some insurers. I prefer them to "going barefoot."

The common alternative to an immediate (distribution) annuity is the deferred type. Income begins later for investments made now. In effect, the assets you place in an annuity grow or pile up income tax-deferred until your retirement or some other agreed-upon date. Only then do payments to the annuitant commence.

The variable type of annuity is a growth investment covered in Chapter Four.

GICs (Guaranteed Insurance Contracts): They're like CDs issued by insurance companies. If secure and well paying, there's no harm in investing in these securities. Retail investors (us) may at times feel a bit sidetracked by their obscurity.

Money markets that pay close to double the inflation rate shouldn't usually tie up more than 10 percent of anyone's financial assets. Six months' living expenses is another conservative guide as to how much belongs in money markets. Even less should be enough. I suggest about 5 percent myself. The millionaire's need for liquidity is low enough, and his or her borrowing capacity strong enough that the liquidity advantage of money markets remains non too attractive.

Mutual funds are media darlings. They're simple. They advertise unstintingly. Galbraith observed that financial genius is a short memory and a rising market. This couldn't apply more perfectly than to the popinjays producing "investment" columns and articles that deal with mutual funds.

Newspapers, magazines, radio and television want to be your financial adviser, not just your doctor, lawyer, poly-sci professor and shrink. They play hackneyed tunes of fear and greed against a background of urgent "discoveries" and "exposes." Like novice food critics reviewing TV dinners, they add little or no value to decision making.

It is definitely true, however, that mutual funds can deliver income well and efficiently in most cases. Their inherent pluses are diversification, convenience and professional management. The tax problem of having your assets in a fund traded willy-nilly doesn't really disadvantage income funds the way it does growth funds.

If you can handle not ever having a specific maturity date and thus no real promise of your investment maintaining its original value, don't avoid funds. They can go up in value too. And remember that, in a mutual fund, the amount of income may be predictable, but it can never be frozen permanently.

Most tax law changes being debated will benefit financial assets as a rule. The proposals have a back-page agenda of encouraging Americans to fund their own retirement. Expected to edge up is the savings rate, which provides capital for national economic expansion.

Private lending to friends and relatives I find an attractive way to earn high returns. The interest you will charge, say from 5 percent up to 18 percent, is justified because you can consider yourself the lender of last resort. Usually you don't make lending too long term to begin with. I myself would rather extend a loan's due date at that time. Or the borrower with your consent may delay scheduled payments in the future if everything remains copasetic.

It's naive to fear that loans between friends or family

members can't work out. The secret is keep it professional. A formal loan agreement (promissory note) prepared or evaluated by a lawyer has to be the first step. Lay out the payment dates. Specify the interest and any special conditions. If all this is new to you and you don't have a lawyer handy, use as a guide one of the commercial forms sold in large office supply stores, like Staples. Importantly, have the lawyer encumber an asset, usually real property, as security for the loan. The borrower doesn't repay what he or she owes in a timely, orderly manner? Then you own the property, the distress sale price of which ought to exceed the amount of the loan.

Forgiving a loan, just letting it go, will always be a subtle sort of gifting. It's your decision, but be prepared. You may really not wish to play for keeps by taking collateral away from the borrower. Having to put up collateral, let's not forget, forces the borrower to consider what he's doing very carefully. If you simply must maintain the income that would be lost through default or a "gift," don't hesitate to foreclose as it were on the asset serving as security. Or you could provide in advance to sell the promissory note for collection by others. In exchange for a discount on its face value, the loan will be out of your hands.

Another wrinkle: For loans larger than $10,000 the Internal Revenue Service "imputes" income to the lender. No sweetheart deals go through. Taxes, interest on the taxes and even penalties can result if you don't treat the assumed interest as income. Before we leave the topic of income pure and simple, let's refresh a perception most of us may carry in our bones. You can't nail down absolute stability of principal, or non-volatility, in a long-term higher-income vehicle. Conversely, you can't get *income* stability *without* going long term. In other words, to really lock in a rate, the "investment" used must take a long time to mature. During this period its resale value will fluctuate, usually in the opposite direction from what's happening in the interest rate environment. When rates generally go down, values generally go up, and of course the reverse is true. Rates and values move in opposite directions. As investors don't usually want either extreme, bonds should be stacked up in a mix or succession of maturities. This way you're not trapped in too much of one thing if the market temporarily moves against you.

Growth of Income

What is the most neglected investment goal? Growth of income. Professionals who design securities portfolios for middle-income people often must allow for maximum income from the start. That's really too bad. People who survive to retirement age can now expect actuarially to live well into their 70s, 80s and 90s. Long-term investing isn't enough. We're going to need ultralong-term.

The specific problem we'll eventually confront in a pure income portfolio is cutbacks in buying power. That is, we'll experience buying power erosion unless we achieve growth of income. Fairly low inflation can still compound to slice a dollar's worth by half in a decade-and-a-half or less. Think back on the successive prices of automobiles you've bought to see how prices double, triple and double again.

Social Security does confer yearly cost of living increases. Its administrators will eventually "means test" payments. Most of us in the field assume payments to millionaires may well be eliminated. Think safety net. It won't be a pension as we understand the term. Yes, the disabled will be paid, along with some of the very elderly.

We'll have to derive income growth from common stocks. Rental property with consistent rent increases can help too. Public limited partnerships always exist that promise to distribute more and more during their operating cycles. Best bet: Don't buy public limited partnership participations period. No means of investing has seemed so discredited recently. Limited partnerships have been described as the orderly conversion of investor assets into fee and commission dollars. Final proof for me of their treachery was a *Wall Street Journal* article in March 1995. Titled "Partnerships, Often Old Dogs, Are Biting Heirs." It told of the myriad problems beneficiaries of deceased limited partners can face. I guess it can be like inheriting a toxic-waste dump.

"Master" limited partnerships, traded on exchanges, incidentally, are an entirely different matter. They include quite superior investments.

Ideally, seekers of income growth buy shares in well-run companies that may be mature, such as utilities, or perhaps have growth capability. Obviously a mature company most likely mails most of its earnings out in dividend checks. Only rarely do mature companies aggressively seek markets or spend heavily on research and development. A growing company, on the other hand, should see such investments pay off in higher earnings, which may result in steeper angles of divided increase (income growth to shareholders). Deferred gratification promises more total gratification over the years.

Aside from common stock, real estate seems to me the only other conventional asset category that has out paced inflation. While inflation over the decades may have averaged only slightly above 3 percent, I've seen figures placing real estate's performance at about 8.5 percent a year.

I hate to skirt the complex topic of personal real estate. This includes renting vs. buying, with the former now seen as sensible. In August 1994 the *New York Times* made a comparison between renting and owning in New York City and San Francisco. Buying won clearly in New York; renting in San Francisco. To do this yourself, total out the entire cost of renting for the period you expect to be there. Then add the figures for buying for the same period. Don't leave anything out. The rollover rule and tax consequences, present and future, touch almost everyone's budget, too.

Right now, though, the discussion we need to get back to centers on owning property the rent from which can be increased to tenants consistently. In other words, growth of income from direct ownership of rental property, residential or commercial. It's not about where and how we ourselves live.

In the negative column are several aggravations. Like

other assets, real estate sees its value fluctuate alarmingly over decades. However, patience, we have learned, paid off most of the time in the past. Unlike some other markets, the real estate market is illiquid. You can't get in and out fast. Spreads between what you have to pay and what you can get if selling look excessive, at least to non-professionals.

Notorious are the difficulties peculiar to real estate. Hassles with tenants often top the list. Next come the unpredictable ingredients of real estate carrying costs. Taxes, maintenance and upkeep and insurance can gyrate. There's the risk of natural disaster and the fact that as an owner you stick out as a potential target of liability lawsuits.

On the positive side there are special satisfactions in owning a tangible income producer. And you'll certainly not have spare time on your hands if you don't delegate all property management. Compensating for risk, effort and aggravation is rental income that can be increased, let's hope, at least as fast as cost of living increases if not more. We may not end up with several points a year in constant appreciation. It's not, however, unreasonable to expect it. Construction peaked in 1988. As vacancies decline values of buildings should continue to firm.

What would tax-reform do to real estate values? By extending depreciation schedules, Tax Equity and Fiscal Responsibility Act in 1986 was heavily responsible for real estate's slide that started in 1988. What about home mortgage deductibility? Some of the reforms now urged could result, through devaluing or eliminating deductibility, in a general decline in real estate value later in this century.

Private real estate investments aren't the easiest way to secure a stream of rising income from the sector. The easiest way is through Real Estate Investment Trusts (REITs). In asset class lexicon *equity REIT* means this: a conduit by which rental income from a real estate portfolio is distributed to shareholders in the form of dividends. It may help to think of a REIT almost as a mutual fund of properties. Unlike mutual funds, however, REITs are fully integrated operating companies. Like mutual funds, REITs buy properties instead of stocks to generate returns.

Again, as with mutual funds and I promise to drop this comparison now, REITs are more diversified as to type than one can first imagine. I know of over 300 separate REITs. Functionally, many concentrate on shopping centers, nursing homes, storage units, trailer parks, office buildings, garden apartments, limited-service hotels or any wedge of the real estate pie you can think of. Geographically, trust managers may select Washington, D.C. (I am not making this up), California, the Southeast or wherever. Apartments in the Southwest and Northwest (Security Capital Property Trust) or the South Atlantic states (United Dominion Realty) have proved a logical choice for increases in both rent and building value.

After all is said and done, good REITs are ultimately paying out about 85 percent of their income. As with utilities, it's usually best to choose REITs with a yield close to or under the long-term Treasury bond rate. Those that pay more (10 percent is available) prove much less likely to appreciate and maintain, much less elevate, their dividend rate. REITs trade on exchanges, usually between $15 and $30 a share. While never as exciting or capable of making a killing as private individual investments, they are no trouble, for one thing. For another, they shrink the chances of irrecoverable loss.

Direct investment, I reckon, means buying into businesses or deals or "situations" that aren't publicly available. For all I know, these private investments may be more important to the country than the openly traded securities we've been more focused on.

Sometimes private banks or investors approach "clients" only to have them lack the know-how to size up an opportunity. Not only is real estate a commonplace part of these proposals, it may be an underlying attraction in other deals. Someone's raising money to buy a fish cannery on an inlet, let's suppose, but only to convert the factory into waterside condos with environmental constraints finessed in advance. Or someone else buys property because it's known that a third buyer is very interested. In the 1970s and 1980s buying and reselling almost simultaneously (flipping the contract) may have been ostensibly a real estate matter. Really it was a short-term money thing. Today, ski and golf developments concern selling real estate, not doing sports.

Sophisticated trust departments may want to put you into oil and gas, venture capital, and leveraged buyouts. With oil and gas you may choose exploration for the big payoff, if not the big bust. Or you could choose royalties or other participation in developed wells or fields. Your income would rise if petroleum prices increase (we can always hope). Sooner or later the planet will run low on oil, but now it looks like the 22nd not the 21st century. Running low isn't the only reason oil prices can go up, but the law of supply and demand won't be repealed.

Royalty trusts use public markets and pay regularly but still enjoy such benefits of direct ownership as tax deductions and special credits. Section 29 Tax Credits, one of the last tax shelters, offer a dollar-for-dollar reduction in income tax liabilities. And two companies, Eastern American Natural Gas and Santa Fe Energy Trust, issue Secured Principal Energy Receipts (SPERs). They use Treasury zero-coupon bonds to assure return of principal eventually. They're speculative, of course, but not extremely so. Chapter Four reopens this subject.

Venture capital usually belongs more to a discussion of speculation or appreciation. Listen carefully, though, to any proposals that convincingly point to producing a steadily increasing income stream. The rule is never to commit more than 10 percent of financial assets to a "venture." Five percent is even better. Venture capital remains a rough game. At the start the dealmakers have the experience and investors the money. Later, the dealmakers can have the money and investors the experience.

One seductive but difficult to categorize investment is the small or perhaps family (probably not your family) business. Once under your control a small company can pay owners salaries that increase consistently. Little work needs to be done to take home those salaries if the business can afford them. And, let's not forget, you're an investor supervising or influencing financial practices, such as who gets paid how much.

How do you find a business of this type? First, if you already own a profitable small business, be wary of selling it. To take part in this world as a newcomer, make friends with those accountants, lawyers, real estate agents, town officials, bankers or brokers who play in this sometimes cozy game. I've never known a community where qualified investors didn't receive a warm welcome. You can be extremely choosy, even picky. That's usually part of the minuet.

Don't forget to ask for and triple-check references from the agent, who may be the seller's attorney. If it's your old community, maybe you can soft-pedal reference checking. Otherwise, err on the cautious side. Be highly specific as to your objective. This section of *What To Do* deals with income growth. As an individual you may also want tax sheltering, property speculation, who knows? Work backward from your objective, not forward, from whatever business is for sale.

Don't be like those couples who relocate to resort areas or college towns and sink everything into an old inn, canoe factory, proprietary school or newspaper. Treat this investment as part of an asset mix. Never put over one-third of your money into a small business if you're a millionaire.

It will be educational, not to mention backbone-stiffening, to absorb and digest the business plan. Use common sense and life experience to reality-check this document. Does the budget seem right? Ask 1,000 questions – you're in charge.

Because the most common cause of small-business failure is undercapitalization, pay close attention to projected "capital needs" figures. Hire experts to analyze building conditions, to determine replacement timing of computers or machine tools, or perhaps to research retail trends. You may not realize that you face, for example, expensive remodeling or an environmental cleanup. With the right attitude all this inconvenience can be fun. Try to convert inconvenience into an adventure. But fun or not, conducting "due diligence" is key. Request any information that will make you comfortable with closing on the acquisition. And prepare yourself for a six-to-12 month process in all but the simplest cases. Patience and detective work today make for a happier tomorrow. What acquirers of small business don't know always costs them.

Retirement Distribution Fine Points

"How to take what you want and need" – indeed. People really need a how-to on retirement distributions. Strategies exist that allow distributions from Individual Retirement Accounts (IRAs) to be stretched out over the lifetime of a very young "non-spousal" beneficiary, even a child. A controversy about whether income taxes are due at death on these yet-to-be-distributed-to-the-beneficiary assets has been reported in the press. As one lawyer was quoted in the *New York Times*, "The rules are very arcane, and the relevant sections of the code are cryptically written." Sounds ominous. Lawyers I checked with randomly, however, believe that it's only estate tax that must be paid at the end of the IRA holder's life if the beneficiary is non-spousal. It is a tremendous break for an heir when income taxes on the assets distributed from the IRA are thus due only as the money comes out over the years. That person who may have 30, 40, 50 years to take out minimal amounts. The bulk of the assets in the IRA could grow hugely during that period while protected from taxation.

If you wish to spend substantial assets from the IRA on yourself, that's another matter. But aside from the few percent mandatory annual withdrawal once the holder reaches age 70 1/2, this could be a way for substantial assets to escape probate (though not estate tax) if that is desired.

What's the problem? It's a fact that a "non-spousal beneficiary may not roll ... retirement assets over into an IRA." The quote is from a respected investment house that acts as an IRA custodian. The same piece of literature continues, however, that the non-spousal beneficiary may withdraw all the inherited money *over his or her own life expectancy* only if he or she acts by the end of the first full calendar following the year of the holder's death. There's no rollover, because the original IRA endures.

The last thing I want to do is pose as someone who can interpret tax law. But if your advisers agree it's doable, this maneuver could shield major amounts of money from the IRS.

Moving to the mundane from the exotic, many retirement plans let participants take their plan balances as a lump sum. Or you can roll these funds over into an IRA, of course. If you take the lump sum, taxes must be paid. The "forward averaging" method lets you take all the money now but calculate the taxes due as if they were on withdrawals paid out over either five-or-10 years. Rule of thumb: Small distributors fare better from a tax standpoint when you choose the 10-year option. That's because 1986 rates, which ten-year averaging uses, peaked at 50 percent. The larger the distribution the more favorable five-year averaging may appear. The reason is that today's rates instead of 1986's have to be used with five-year averaging.

Let's digress to the subject of penalty-free withdrawal from IRAs before the age of 59 1/2. I'm not talking about hardships, death or disability. I'm referring to a stream of annuitized payments. Annuitization requires that roughly equal withdrawals occur at least once a year. This can go on as long as you or your designated beneficiary lives.

Most people aren't aware that you don't have to be 59 1/2 to "take what you want and need" from your IRA. But three different annuitization patterns are possible. You do have to accept being tied to a payment scheme until five years pass or you reach age 59 1/2. That shouldn't be a headache if you want significant drawdowns.

Let's review the Required Minimum Distribution (RMD) method first. Each year you divide your IRA account balance by your single or joint life expectancy. You may use, and many do, the *recalculating* method for succeeding years. Just use your new life-expectancy figure each year. Another RMD option is the *declining years* technique. The first year, use the life-expectancy table. After that just take away one year each year from your life expectancy. As you can see the yearly payout to you would vary somewhat.

The amortization method tries to reduce the IRA balance to zero at your death. Whenever distributions start, a credible interest rate is assumed. It's like a mortgage that way. Unlike the RMD, withdrawal amounts don't change.

Neither do withdrawals vary if you select the third option, which is to use an *annuity factor*. Using the IRS life-expectancy chart you divide the IRA balance by this number called an annuity factor. It's derived from mortality statistics. Like the amortization method just described, it theoretically aims to reduce your balance to zero over your remaining lifetime.

When you attain 59 1/2 you can stop using methods you chose and essentially do whatever you want to with the money. Income tax, remember, is paid on withdrawals.

Which is for you? Annuity Factor takes out most and RMD the least. Here's a comparative example on a $500,000 IRA for a 50-year-old. Under the RMD method, using recalculation the first annual distribution is $15,105. The second year its $16,265. For purposes of this comparison I'm assuming an 8 percent return.

Using the amortization method, the annual distribution comes to $43,395. The annuity factor way produces

$45,010. Amortization and annuity factor distributions are fixed at the same amount each year for five years or until you're 59 1/2, remember. For this reason fewer people choose the RMD. It's essentially unpredictable.

Invading Capital

"Thou shalt not invade thy capital" is practically the 11th Commandment in some financial cultures. Whether or not the United States has in fact witnessed the "development of a hereditary aristocracy of wealth" or not, to cite James Bryant Conant, we automatically think that the more we leave our families the better.

Much reasoning can challenge this mind-set. Foremost is the belief that our first responsibility is to ourselves. Some people believe this therapeutic age tenet. Others don't.

The next chapter investigates the objective of dying poor. That means having your assets run out about the time your life does. It's probably worth a separate book. What "invading principal" refers to, however, is the necessary or wisely advised or carefully considered use of capital itself to further goals, improve one's living, ease discomfort, help others, you name it. It has no goal (though perhaps the result) of getting rid of all one's money over time.

At the opposing edge of the spectrum from dying-poor people stand those whose deny themselves everything it seems, even necessities. The purpose is to minimize spending and maximize savings. Often these types of people don't even recognize their own "rainy day."

Rainy day, as in what we've allegedly been saving for.

My advice adds up to this: Carve the emotion and unwarranted fear out of decisions to invade or preserve principal. The best way is numerical analysis. That's a fancy way of saying do the numbers. Following are some precise calculations (no guesswork) as to how long it would take to exhaust a sum of money by taking out more income than the sum earns.

For illustrative uses, let's assume a conservative total return (income and growth) of 8 percent. If we figure arbitrarily on $500,000 of principal, the annual income is $40,000. If you needed $50,000 income from this $500,000 the rate would be 10 percent, wouldn't it? Taking 10 percent from a sum earning only 8 percent requires 20.2 years to deplete the entire amount.

If you took out $45,000, or 9 percent, the number of years is 27.6.

We'd like to assume an annual total return of at least 10 percent over the decades, though. If we achieved that, there would be no drawing down of the principal in the first example. So, if you wanted $55,000 a year, or 11 percent, on the $500,000, it would take 24.1 years of invading principal with the annual return 10 percent. Taking out $55,000 while earning only 8 percent, or $40,000, you would run out of money in 16.3 years.

Obviously money lasts indefinitely if our earnings rate equals or exceeds the payout rate. But because we are speaking of invading principal, let's run a couple of extreme examples. Suppose you take $100,000 a year in income but earned only 10 percent, or $50,000, seven years would go by before the last of the principal vaporized. If you earned 15 percent, it will last 9.3 years.

That's one way of invading capital. Just as common seems the direct withdrawal of major chunks of principal at one time instead of regularly enhancing income. The first calculus should probably be, "What does this do to my income?" If it can be foregone, splendid. If not, what juggling of which assets will reduce the income shortfall? Must new risks be incurred? What is the "time horizon"? If any doubts find satisfactory resolutions, if invading principal simply requires strategic jiggering, my advice is forget the 11th Commandment. Invent your own. How about "Forsake rigidity if life itself suffers."

Changing Countries

Another ancient injunction could be, "Lead us not into taxation." Readers have disparate views on "revenue." In 1993, the last year for which I know the figures, the top 1 percent of taxpayers, by income, paid almost 30 percent of federal taxes. In a number of cases, people have given up U.S. citizenship to avoid taxes here that they regard as confiscatory. Working abroad for the U.S. State Department, I encountered "expats" 30 years ago. In the 1970s my own accountant suggested Liechtenstein residence and presumably citizenship. For me, a pretty small fish.

There are lots of prominent people who leave the United States officially. I remember John Huston and William Holden when I was young. Recently, owners of Campbell Soup, Dart Container, Carnival Cruise Lines and Duty Free Shoppers and other big outfits have hit the headlines for leaving our tax system behind.

Our tax code is unusual in that no matter where U.S. citizens are, our taxes apply. In most countries tax authorities cut nationals a lot of slack if they live away from their homeland. We do the opposite.

My embassy experience has conclusively dissuaded me from the idea of surrendering U.S. citizenship. The first reason is that getting it back is shockingly difficult and chancy. The second is that Internal Revenue will apply levies to your holdings for another 10 years when they have a suspicion that your motive in leaving was to avoid paying taxes.

If you think that the end of the Cold War and the governmentalizing of American life erode the benefits of citizenship here, there are many other choices. Switzerland, Ireland, Israel and Canada (which has no estate tax) remain obvious old favorites. For the last few decades many warm-islands nations provide tax-favored safe harbors. The Bahamas, Caymans, and Bermuda attract huddled masses yearning to earn free. The British Virgins, Belize, Turks and Caicos and St. Kitts-Nevis are newly popular. St. Kitts-Nevis is known for neither income nor estate taxes.

Hardly anyone I know would seriously envision giving up American citizenship. On the contrary, it seems as if the whole world is trying to move here, not leave. But if you are serious I would gather precise information. Perhaps start with an international law firm such as Cadwalader Wickersham & Taft in New York. Your own lawyer can help you find somebody. Or an international Big Six accounting organization like Price Waterhouse.

First for me would be relaxed visits to any place I might call home, even if it's to be little more than a mail drop in my future. If it's Bermuda, for example, visit some trust companies and law offices that serve mainland referrals. Offshore firms have U.S. correspondents.

*   *   *

Short answer: Nail down income and growth-of-income needs before you relax. Put the bulk of your money in predictable mainstream instruments you understand.

Chapter Four

Should I Die Poor?

> "There is, I think, an essential difference of character in mankind, between those who wish to do, and those who wish to have certain things."
>
> – William Hazlitt (1778-1830)

Financial advice too often arrives in the absence of serious value judgments. Financial advice usually reflects little awareness of people's roots. Financial advice exists in a world nearly empty of culture, history, family, philosophy, religion. Mostly it's a base commodity. Not without important uses, for sure, but largely shallow and hollow beyond the obvious.

An interesting exception, at least the beginnings of one, may be the current debate between estate planning and anti-inheritance planning. Traditionally, responsible asset holders, on reaching middle age, make estate arrangements. They consult books, accountants, salesmen, legal counsel, their own family and charities. They attend seminars and talk to trust departments. The typical outcome is a series of documents that give part away (Chapter Five) and pass the rest on to others (Chapter Six). Poised against this viewpoint is the bumper sticker "I'm spending my children's inheritance" or the poster "Fly first class. Your children will." These exhortations sound vaguely hedonistic the first time we see them. But at the same time there's an inarguable quality there, isn't there?

At least on first glance. You worked for it; now let it work for you.

That said, though, what purpose does dying poor serve? What's good about it? The first thing that may pop into our minds is "You can't take it with you" anyway. Or the Bible warning, "it's harder for a camel to pass through the eye of a needle than for a rich man to enter the kingdom of heaven." The lessons here about the futility of dying rich may not be the primary lessons intended. And they may not apply to your circumstances. But we grew up in a culture that underneath it all stresses that, in that line of *Barry Lyndon*, "all is dust."

Long after that was written, a 20th-century trend in underlying values has eclipsed another long-lived way of perpetuating family prosperity. This eclipsed tradition was for property or an established business or some way of continuing the family's living to be passed on to the young. Except for a thin layer of top-shelf dynasties, the handing down of significant money itself, just plain money, has not been a terribly widespread phenomenon for too long. Part of this of course has to do with the huge portion of citizens who used to live on family farms. They've dwindled to a fingernail paring of the populace now.

The new trend is for knowledge and skills to constitute ultimate wealth, rather than dollars and yen. In the sense of our subject here, brains will never replace dollars exactly. It is the knowledge society, however, or age of information or transformation or whatever you call it today. What you know and can do will come to be relatively more valuable vis-à-vis monetary worth than it is now.

This is the trend if not yet the reality. Thus helping pay for the upcoming generation to acquire these needed abilities may prove more helpful in the long run to them than their receiving a legacy of money later in life. The givers, ourselves, will experience emotional and intellectual benefits that come from helping others while we're alive to witness the results.

It's known that the gift tax favors receivers of gifts more than estate taxes favor heirs. How can this be if rates for gift and estate taxes are the same? The trick is that a given sum to be received is taxed to the giver at a lower effective rate than it is to the deceased's estate. An extreme example may help clear this up. You want $250,000 to go to a nephew after taxes. You're facing, in this illustration, the same maximum bracket (60 percent) whether it's a gift or inheritance. As a gift you would use up $400,000: $250,000 to the nephew and $150,000 to the IRS. By contrast, if you left $400,000 to the nephew the IRS would take 60 percent or $240,000. The nephew would receive only $160,000. Is this the revenge of the nerds or what? To accomplish your original intent of transferring $250,000 after taxes to your nephew, you would have to leave him $625,000. Your money would be $625,000 smaller instead of $400,000 smaller.

There's nothing we can do about it, but three years have to elapse between the gift and your death. If not the IRS refigures your taxes as if you had bequeathed. Not only can we enjoy watching others spend our money, but surprise! We can enjoy freer spending on ourselves. Certainly things like housekeeping assistance, massage therapy, commodious lodging when traveling, a thousand things, can make life easier to take. Remodeling for comfort, keeping horses or boats, golf club membership, plastic surgery, hiring limousines instead of driving – these luxuries are rarely burdensome. In today's world especially, good causes need help more and more. Starting with your own church, synagogue, museum, library, hospital, orchestra, school, or public broadcaster, we can climb the ladder from local up to national not-for-profits. Don't rule out a gift to an individual where it would make a real difference. What's that saying? "Commit random acts of senseless kindness"?

Dying poor lets us undo any damage done from having admitted crass business world values into our personal lives. The cynical tag line "Who dies with the most toys wins" can stand for precisely what anti-inheritance planning opposes. The tendencies to chisel, to dissemble, always to put oneself first, to cheat when no one's looking, all suddenly seem quite pointless. If you're not plotting to pad your final financial score, then what's the point? The point of not being your best self? A bleak last line on an epitaph in Stowe reads, "No one cares but you." That certainly applies to estate size more than millionaires like to think.

What's Wrong with Dying Poor?

If using up and giving away our resources while we're still alive has all these advantages, then, what's wrong with doing that? Quite a few minuses do in fact attach themselves to the anti-inheritance-planning minimovement idea, it turns out.

The ordinary affluent American, as Dr. Thomas Stanley's studies show clearly, isn't comfortable with "upshifting." This refers to spending measurably more on living expenses than you had planned. Not only can it prove embarrassing, but it's often just plain hard. Imagine supervising a household staff, to conjure up an extreme example. The Southern phrase "getting above your raising" implies criticism for "putting on airs." The sheer god-awful "shadow work," in Ivan Ilyich's phrase, of expanding your shopping universe daunts many. Shadow work is the stuff like shopping and cleaning and preparing tax returns and so on that you have to do but don't get paid for. The point is only that much of what we think will improve life only clutters it.

Another thing that will appear wrong to many is the way spending all your money defies common sense. Poetic immortality, creating a work of art that survives us, has been a given in human society for millennia. The theory of parental investment credibly holds that our dominant biological urge is to place our genes into succeeding generations. So why should money be different? Why wouldn't we wait to accumulate estate assets for maximum impact and usefulness after death.

Being urged by self-appointed authorities to divest assets raises other questions. Who are these people? Who needs the voice of authority for every personal element of life? Arc we in danger of losing our ability to make such important basic decisions? Without advice, solicited or not?

Commentators and shade-tree psychologists always urge us to put ourselves first. Well-known authors like Ayn Rand show philosophical innocence on this question. We ultimately do what we want to do by definition. Even Mother Theresa's altruism reflects her own personal inner beliefs and desires. The point here is that if our practice is to squirrel away pennies and save string so that our assets grow, then that's what we want to do. I've always heard that trying to change someone who doesn't want to change is a hostile act anyway.

Investment counselor, writer and financial phrasemaker John Train has weighed in on the question of unearned riches. "Excess wealth is a fatal disincentive to a productive life." More than one academic study shows that inheritance, even the prospect of inheritance, can diminish an individual's work ethic. Personal planning and activities involving money don't seem as important when a bequest could bail us out. So that means you're not necessarily doing heirs a favor by arranging bigger inheritances, doesn't it? Well, only if you accept the view that a strong work ethic and careful budgeting and so on are important. I may think they are, you may be sure they are, experts "know" they are. But what if they're only a step along the way between the worms and stars? Like hand-to-hand combat ability, or the know how to make your own cheese? Or build a canoe? What if they're only options – one way to live – one set of emphases.

Some of my World War II veteran neighbors when I

was growing up disparaged the fighting spirit and ability of the armed forces of France and Italy. I made similar observations in South Vietnam. Nagging at me even then, though, was a suspicion that ineffectiveness in battle and a general lack of enthusiasm about fighting may be in some senses a virtue. Someone who "stops and smells the roses" just may be higher on the monkey bars than the power-walking pursuer of shorter commute times.

I'm digressing to make the point that unexamined values could be behind the implication that inheritance has negative effects. I'll concede the effects, but not necessarily that they're always negative.

People in my business have to read a lot. Not that all of us do. But many of us note tendencies in the print media, and television is even more blatant, that persist over the years. One thing is the bias toward consumption.

No matter how forward thinking the *Post*, *Globe*, or *Chronicle* wish to appear, they only occasionally drop their persistent urgings to try this, buy that, go here, improve this, make that, learn this, eat that, experience this, try anything, especially if it costs money. Naturally, spending your money soon is what makes sense to opinion makers, especially if some of the recipients are advertisers. Journalists don't even do this deliberately. It's just an inextricable part of the commercial media mix.

Even the push by the press to support euthanasia and assisted suicide could stem partially, it has been devilishly suggested, from the perhaps unaware cravings of baby boomers for the assets of the nearly deceased.

My opinion is that in a commercial democracy such

as ours, the dominant approach urged for almost everything is a form of shopping. This way, you see, we need experts to guide us. Unhappy with your religion? Shop around. Bored with your spouse? Watch TV for clues as to how to act. Don't like Congress? Shop for new members. Just sitting on your money? Start spending now, while spry. I see the "dying broke" vision as one more idea to buy. Which of course doesn't mean it's wrong. But we must remember that it's only a point of view. There are many in today's shopping mall of ideas.

Is there a serious underlying school of thought, even a seminal thinker or two behind dying poor? If so, they're well hidden. The reason I ask is that the advocates of a major shift in public attitudes could prove no wiser than sincere snake oil salespersons. Remember the first Dr. Atkins diet? Eat fat and grow healthy. In finance there's always a Howard Ruff or Joe Granville, frequently wrong but never in doubt. Henry Kaufman and Paul Erdman may have doctorates. But have they made any predictions that panned out? What they do have is an absolute assuredness of manner and – frequently – good tailoring. The point is that there's always a surfeit of free advice that won't work out. There's plenty of paid advice like that, too.

The last point I'll raise that makes me wary is the use of paradox. My Random House dictionary defines paradox this way: "1. a statement or proposition seemingly contradictory or absurd but in reality expressing a possible truth. 2. a self-contradictory or false proposition." And so forth. If there ever was a world rife with paradoxical advice it's the world of money. Could it be that the advice to give away or spend all your money is just an inversion of reality? Combine easy paradoxicalism (my coinage) with the journalistic assumption that nothing is what it seems and you could come up with a mischievous recipe for misery. But that, too, would be only a point of view.

The last negative thing to mention about dying poor is the loss of "stepped-up basis." When assets instead of being inherited are received as gifts, any change in value is calculated from the giver's cost, or "basis." When assets are inherited the basis, or point of calculation, is the value at the deceased person's death. Or you may choose to use the date six months after death. So what? Well, it's a pretty big deal.

Let's say Exxon stock has a cost basis for the gift giver of $3 a share. That becomes the recipient's cost basis. If the stock is sold, capital gains tax is applied to the difference between $3 and say $73 a share. That's huge. If the stock were inherited, the cost basis at death might be $65 or $75 a share. Vastly better from the taxable-gains perspective.

It's axiomatic that tax considerations alone shouldn't govern a grand investment strategy. Something as hugely important as the stepped-up basis at death will certainly remain influential until laws are revised, if ever. Capital gains, in other words, would be much greater on received instead of inherited assets. At the time of liquidation of a low-cost-basis gifted asset, the owner thus faces greater taxation.

Asset Transfer Effects

We've touched on the effect a windfall could create for the recipients. They may be heirs or other individuals. Recipients may be not-for-profit entities of any sort. And don't forget that bequests go to taxed for-profit organizations as well.

Suppose that, like a good many of my clients, you have no heirs. Perhaps you outlived all those close to you. Or those of your friends and family surviving may possess vastly more wealth than you. Then you don't have any valid concern about the relative effect of gifts vs. inheritances.

Your own attitude toward charity, if you're typical, is flexible. Politically, conservatives like the idea of private financing of good works. They tend to see government programs as potential wasters of funds coercively extracted. Liberals see private money behind the great progressive institutions of the 20th century: universities and foundations. They want generous contributing to environmental lobbies, civil rights causes, non-mainstream culture and the like.

Sometimes your only question is do I give to charity now or later. If now, you get tax deductions, estate size reduction and perhaps a greater role in how the organization applies your donation, what it's spent for. If you plan to do it at death, you may face years of worshipful attention from fund-raisers. With certain types of giving you receive the tax deduction now. But the money can pay, if you like, for an income stream to you. This stream could in fact work to deplete the gift. A warehouse-sized loophole may permit you to reduce the assets of your gift through withdrawals without revising the amount you deducted from taxes.

The charity's attitude is to welcome gifts now and future. Gifts accrue on various timetables. The money you leave will be needed often as much or more than the money you may have given years earlier.

As to transferring assets before death to individuals, most often family members, let's ponder some positive and negative effects. If you plan to die poor, you would tend to spend more on "heirs" sooner, say on valuable education. You would have removed comfort-cushion or slacker-mentality "enabling" by making it clear that those following you must essentially make it on their own. Their survival priorities should improve. Their self-reliance should grow.

Legacies may eat away at work values – we know this anecdotally. A 1992 study of IRS data in fact determined that almost 20 percent of people who inherited $150,000 or more quit working. Two years later a professor at Brown discovered that, within a given income bracket, those expecting to inherit don't save as much as, but do spend more than, those who think they will not be left anything by others. Is anyone shocked?

Inheritances cause misunderstandings, wounded feelings and resentment. Unfairness is frequently perceived. Relationships suffer. "Where there's a will, there's a relative" we've seen embroidered on novelty pillows. In my family, my wife's family and in the families of many of our acquaintances, we can list incidents where people may go decades nursing an estate-related hurt. People in close families wind up no longer on speaking terms. To tell the truth, there is a seeming surplus of unintentional injustice in the inheritance business. Even if there weren't, the apparent capriciousness too often packed into wills and trusts is enough to ignite a family world war.

Wouldn't the dying-poor choice alleviate some of the domestic disturbances caused by inheritances? You'd be alive to deal with imbalances, unfairness and favoritism. It's a happy thought. Common sense says if you wait until you're dead, there's not any useful way to learn that your approach could tear apart your family. If you give assets away during your life, people may speak up. You then decide whether you lean too much one way and not the other. Whether you "just don't get it."

Personal budgeting and financial planning suffer if instead of receiving gifts along the way we drift about like Prince Charles waiting for our benefactor to die. I had an acquaintance who embodied fiscal imprudence. It turned out that she was just waiting for her chain-smoking in-law to leave a seven-figure balance behind.

My friend, in her 40s, took two-hour lunches, drove expensive cars hard, built a mansion in the woods, neglected her job, and involved himself in questionable schemes abroad and in far corners of the United States. It wouldn't be hard to prove that her immaturity, actually arrested development, grew from her awareness that the expected legacy would dwarf any likely consequences of carefully managing her money today. Guess what? Divorce. Just a coincidence, probably, but one that happens to many. I think that judicious gifting practices by the in law would have lessened negative externalities in this case. Money given in view of the donor isn't apt to bc squandered. As in the Old Testament story of the talents, it isn't likely to be buried unproductively either.

The dying-poor plan in essence relieves giftees of strains from leading an undercapitalized life. It should add muscle to prudent money use. Just waiting for money can lead to atrophy in that aspect. In a slightly different key, Edmund Wilson's character learns that there's nothing quite so debilitating as a "small but adequate income."

The sad truth is that manipulativeness with money is usually tolerated. Manipulating people in the heavy-handed controlling sense, though, should be shunned. But conditioning participation in a gifting schedule or program on wise use of the money received can be the best way to handle things.

The deeper we go into the anti-inheritance philosophy and its implications the more we appreciate it. But at the same time our skepticism swells. In this one-hand-vs.-the-other-hand dialogue, let's look at traditional "estate planning:" how we leave things behind when we die. It's good to remember that this tradition isn't rooted very deeply in the middle-class memory bank.

Those of us who may think we can't absorb the pace of change in the Information Age, take heed. In 1915 the largest group of Americans lived on farms. Now productive farmers make up only 2 percent of the work force. That in itself would have caused a cyclone of change in the inheritance arrangements society makes. The next socioeconomic upheaval is beginning to result from the passing on of all the money made and assets appreciated since World War II.

One 1993 investigation calculated that the total amount baby boomers will inherit is about $10.5 million. Another estimate is $8 trillion; another, $12 trillion. Recent and upcoming revision in longevity tables and tax codes undercut any pretense to precision in these figures. But this is the straw stirring the drink of most personal-inheritance planning.

As a comparison benchmark, to interject, all the holdings in America's 6,000 mutual funds total in value about $3 trillion. Three-or-four years ago insurance and investment people would warn us that the $600,000 exclusion from federal gift and estate taxes was in danger. If it declined to $200,000 the national debt could supposedly be retired by taxes on the boomers' legacies. As it happened, Washington has been veering in the other direction. It may raise the $600,000 ($1.2 million per couple) to $750,000 ($1.5 million).

Against the political leveling effect of heavier estate taxation, we note the unsettling vision of families forced to dismantle or liquidate healthy enterprises and farms to pay even today's estate taxes. We see the widening of income and ownership extremes in American society. But suggested "corrective" policies seem to punish prudence and savings. Against the ideal of the "commons" where everyone shares with everyone else via the government or other mechanism, we witness the taking apart piece by piece of key portions of the welfare state.

We hear pleas that we don't do enough. The put-upon rejoinder is "Look at what's left of my paycheck." Not even calculated are the hundreds of other taxes applied to everything we do and own. In other words, this most fundamental of debates will continue to the end of democracy. My own view is that for the next few decades emphasis will be on enabling the middle class to finance its own retirement without funding by the government. You could argue that it's not the middle class who needs the most help. And you could argue back that this will allow government money to go more to the most desperate needy, not the middle class.

At any rate, those who hope to inherit money can operate differently from those getting it now. Other things being equal, prospective heirs should use credit, or deficit financing. Why? A couple of reasons. Credit is the sinew of American commerce, to begin with. Expectant heirs can make especially good use of borrowing: They're probably going to be bailed out anyway. Second, the discipline of borrowing, or on a grand scale, of the "credit markets," is a third eye overseeing our financial conduct.

Expecting a bequest is never a license to waste. But neither should we remain slaves to the benefactor's life span if crucial matters are at stake today. Tuition, business expansion, prolonged unemployment. Hating to use debt and credit can be the socialism of the ignorant.

You won't find many Americans who don't believe that adversity sharpens survival skills. Prosperity seems to dull our wits, appetites, instinct for self-preservation and sharpness with a pencil. Or so we are instructed as regards "easy money."

This disposition of thought is applied to welfare clients at low economic rungs. It goes all the way up to dissipated drug-using aristocrats. If landed lotus eaters were more Spartan and less Athenian, the conventional wisdom intones, society wouldn't be dragged down by their indolence and bad example. I believe this.

But I have to stay on guard against swallowing whole several belief systems that sag under close analysis. For one, people my age were reared in the Great Depression's aftermath. There are those who base everything on Depression-linked learning experiences. They fight the last war and don't prepare for the next. I've heard these people say that giving money to the young "spoils" them.

The flawed cosmos of sports also supplies a set of semiquestionable shibboleths and images. The old honor system is hanging on in some playgrounds and neighborhoods, I imagine. But the dominant ethos in spectator sports is often hypocrisy. What can I get away with? Extroverted toughness replaces self-effacing inner strength and confidence. The macho creed of ostensibly bootstrapping oneself from nowhere argues against getting too much help from others. At least implicitly. Do it yourself and wait patiently for any inheritance that may lie ahead.

The business world, which depends on cooperation, is the source of a sanctioned extreme selfishness. "I've got mine." "What have you done for me lately?" This way of thinking readily laps over into worship of the work ethic and social Darwinism. "Sink or swim." From the giver's side, the crass business view is why on earth would anyone shrink his pile, the measure of achievement. From the recipient side, do the points scored through someone else's kindness even count?

Today's non-stop discussion of large legal questions casts a shadow over personal planning and behavior. Do I weaken myself unforgivably by not staying rich? "He who has the gold makes the rules." I guess you could answer that at least you won't have "deep pockets," which alone could provoke lawsuits. Whatever lessons the course of current legal practice may hold for the dying-poor debate elude me. So far, it's like rare diseases. Fearful and fascinating, they still strike seldom enough that we live life around them. The odds of any of us having our fortunes ruined through quirks in the law is statistically tiny. Just don't be surprised when advised to hang on to every cent "for your own protection."

Because the issue involves money, the temptation exists to "bottom line" everything in financial planning. This is a mistake. Don't take off your human being hat. Don't buy into substitutes for the moral codes that should guide us.

The generation now passing the torch proved that survival skills and traditional work ethics can build a wonderful society. America today for individuals too is a breathtaking product of their industry and improvisational genius. Let's remember first, however, that it's their values and spiritual ideals that will endure, as it is with us. We must avoid personal financial decision-making that excludes the needs of others from the calculation.

One background theme throughout any use of professional advice givers is that many display a tin ear when it comes to hearing inner persons speak. Their gaze may be deep, but their insights shallow. We all know how society esteems the dollar. Love of money runs in the veins of the great majority of those who offer investment counsel. This is worse even than it seems. The importance of money is self-evident. Dwelling on it, like gravity or mortality, rapidly diminishes in utility. When using a tool like money, the tool itself ideally disappears. Money is simply the air we breathe when deciding how we and our heirs or benefactors will arrange affairs. Instead of moving stacks of shekels around, we should leave money decisions until last. We will find money answers staring up at us once we have made life decisions. True, a little professional advice can turn a puzzle into a map. But don't get involved with professionals who have no inkling of who you really are. Especially avoidable are those whose one-dimensional money tail wags the dog.

Socrates is most often quoted that an unexamined life is not worth living. Well, maybe not to him. But examining your life does help enormously when you're setting goals and priorities. You may find that you have neither worked nor played. You have simply done things. Keep this in the forefront of your mind if trying to decide whether to die rich or poor. And make use of this insight should you be trying to figure out if a potential beneficiary has sufficient "work ethic" to deserve some money ahead of time. Successful, happy people, I find, let their activities determine whether they save or spend. It's not usually the other way around.

How to Die Poor

You're intrigued enough, let's assume, that you have already done a dying-poor trial run in your mind. Have you ever, contemplating mortality, figured the year your life might end? I've seen articles and formulas that probably narrow the odds down. A family physician could make a good guess if he or she wanted to. If you have the courage to look into this, and I definitely do not, it might illuminate planning for the next part of your life.

When I first went into securities, there were only a dozen-or-fewer types of things you could do with money. In the late 1980s someone calculated that there were 65. Now it must be a 100. These insurance and investment inventions are like refinements in medicine. You target objectives more precisely nowadays.

Before choosing the way to proceed, we must put numbers on financial needs for when we're living. That done, our personal policies for the future can materialize and pass a reality check at the same time. It's a relief how much vagueness and imprecision can be taken out of your expectations for the future. To reduce uncertainty to zero, we'd have to know the expiration date on your birth certificate. But we can certainly minimize and offset risks to very bearable levels.

Income needs, if you don't know exactly, require someone to do a personal cash-flow analysis. See the Appendix for a helpful form if you could use one. At its most basic, you add all income and subtract all expenses. You'll probably either have too much (called excess) or little (called deficiency). We can gradually let go of assets that yield unneeded income if we like. More subtly, we can use specific techniques to ensure that our necessities will be covered until we die. And we can use specific investments and types of insurance to reduce total holdings but maintain or enhance our way of life.

Suppose you're still on the job. We can calculate the income you'll need the first year of retirement. We'll make use of a compound-interest table (Figure 2). Fill in the blanks:

1. Annual income today ____________
2. Work years left ____________
3. Average annual raise ____________ %
4. Interest table factor* ____________
5. Income at retirement
   (1. times 4.) ____________
6. Income needed
   (75 percent of 5.) ____________

*Use 2. and 3.

Some readers already play with personal financial numbers on their "macroscope" or computer. Others have worked out the outlines, even details of spending policies and practices for upcoming deadlines.

Years	*5%*	*6%*	*7%*	*8%*	*9%*	*10%*
1	1.0500	1.0600	1.0700	1.0800	1.0900	1.1000
2	1.1025	1.1236	1.1449	1.1664	1.1881	1.2100
3	1.1576	1.1910	1.2250	1.2597	1.2950	1.3310
4	1.2155	1.2625	1.3108	1.3605	1.4116	1.4641
5	1.2763	1.3382	1.4026	1.4693	1.5386	1.6105
6	1.3401	1.4185	1.5007	1.5869	1.6771	1.7716
7	1.4071	1.5036	1.6058	1.7138	1.8280	1.9487
8	1.4775	1.5938	1.7182	1.8509	1.9926	2.1436
9	1.5513	1.6895	1.8385	1.9990	2.1719	2.3579
10	1.6289	1.7908	1.9672	2.1589	2.3674	2.5937
11	1.7103	1.8983	2.1049	2.3316	2.5804	2.8531
12	1.7959	2.0122	2.2522	2.5182	2.8127	3.1384
13	1.8856	2.1329	2.4098	2.7196	3.0658	3.4523
14	1.9799	2.2609	2.5785	2.9372	3.3417	3.7975
15	2.0789	2.3966	2.7590	3.1722	3.6425	4.1772

Compound Interest Table
Figure 2

One way or another, let's start by finding out how much we could give away, if any. It's not that we're rushing to the poorhouse. The figure, though, if you're fortunate enough to have one, will inform subsequent thinking on the dying-poor idea.

For the last few years investment companies and financial planners have had software that does all the arithmetic for us. You can typically have these numbers run as an isolated reckoning. The cost of doing so should prove nominal to non-existent. That is, unless you have the financial formulation serve as a centerpiece of an elaborate, detailed many-paged plan.

Once we have a good idea how much our assets exceed "sufficiency," we can spell out our personal policy. I resist harping on the value of putting it in writing. "Easy for you to say," I can hear. Believe me, discomfort is the last thing I want readers to feel. Trust me on this, though. The exercise of writing out your personal guidelines and goals will be revealing and fulfilling. At least give it 20 minutes.

A written policy is a kind of hub stake giving you a way to mark progress. It's good to review how things are going. If change overwhelms you, modify the policy. If you stick to the indicated routes, though, true detours won't often have to be taken.

If you simply can't get started on this, by the way, drop a note to Woodcock Publishing. You will receive some sample formats. If you've committed the basics to writing, you may include your work in progress and pertinent background data for an objective editing.

Insurance

Until the 1970s, it seems to me, the term *major medical* was distinctive. Now it's simply the standard policy. Chief variables in policies of this type are (1) the maximum amount the policies will pay and (2) the amount of deductible and co-insurance you choose. No matter how positive-thinking and even Panglossian you may be, first-rate major medical is a sine qua non of the dying-poor set. Spending insurance dollars that aren't required, though, is as great an error for the affluent as it would be for the impoverished.

Most of us reading this book can afford larger deductibles and co-payments. Don't pay for policies that provide "first dollar" coverage. As there's no disincentive with these policies for holders to run to the doctor with every little thing, insurers and insured are moving away from them. Most illnesses don't really cost that much. Thus insurance companies can afford to grant much lower premiums to those who will in effect pay most of their own bills anyway. Accept the largest deductible you're comfortable with.

As with most things, the rich can take more risk with medical insurance. Because they can afford to pick up tabs themselves, they can act as partial self-insurers for the sake of lower premiums. What we worry about primarily are those not totally commonplace disorders that wipe out what's left of a fortune: the catastrophes. They are the crocodiles in the river of retirement ease. Do make sure that adequate coverage for the "big ones" isn't scanted.

We covered long-term-care insurance starting on page 39. Holding money in reserve for nursing home or home-health expenses, as an alternative to insurance, keeps that money from otherwise being any use to you. For many people, LTC policies simply merit consideration. For people planning to die poor, however, necessity is a much more appropriate way to look at it.

Also refer to page 39 for a brief mention of disability coverage. Added emphasis on disability insurance in a discussion of how to die poor is appropriate for a couple of important reasons. The first is that, even if you're working, you're allotting more money to your family than would otherwise seem prudent. Less savings, in other words. Less safe, though, for your family unless you have disability (while working).

As to life insurance, I find that a lot of people in my generation bought large whole-life policies the same way they may have gone to college or left their hometown to move to a city or even married. The simplest thing to do was just go ahead with it. You believed that a lot of time and mental energy spent analyzing the thing would lead you to the same conclusion. In effect those policies substituted in many cases for the savings programs that invariably seem to work out better. The discipline in paying that premium took the place of the tougher discipline needed to save and invest consistently.

What's the lesson? That buying a prepackaged mass-market solution to life's problems doesn't serve the customer foremost. In most instances, it serves the packager. The quite competitive insurance industry does have perfect products for certain purposes. For example, if you want to give all your money to old Rutgers and still leave your heirs plenty, the wealth-replacement trust, using life insurance, will do the job. If you are planning to die poor, though, it's term insurance you want. Not for your own whole life, certainly, but just to allow for the loss of important income in perhaps middle age caused by the death of a spouse. Once savings are adequate, drop term-life insurance. Relatively inexpensive policies decades hence can cover funeral costs and other sundry postmortem debts.

Gifting

Gifting, in the 1990s and beyond, is such a critical part of *What To Do With A Million Dollars* that I've spent the whole next chapter on it. "Giving Part Away" leans more to traditional estate planning tools. Most of the traditional benefits of giving – tax deductions, estate shrinkage and sometimes increasing your income stream – will also interest those intrigued by the concept of dying poor.

The neatest anti-inheritance tax loophole is the $10,000 annual gift that you can give to anyone at all once a year. For a couple especially, this adds up fast. There are no tax implications at all.

One popular dying-poor option is the benefaction to a not-for-profit organization, often a college. In return for your gift you can be guaranteed an annuity payment for as long as you live. You also get to deduct a large amount from taxes today. Functionally, I think, we should treat this sort of contract as an investment, though it in essence is a gift. It just acts like an investment. Outright donations to charitable organizations lend a sense of fulfillment, of giving back something, to life. That you can be hailed in public while alive is a plus to many but a minus to some, who give huge amounts anonymously.

If you leave all your possessions to charity, no estate tax at all will be owed. More typical is the use of charitable trusts to pass partial bequests on to other beneficiaries. After all, you may not use up every last cent while alive. The Remainder Trust has a feature that makes it easy to remember how it differs from the Income Trust.

The Charitable Remainder Trust can be established at death or during your life. It arranges that a certain amount of income will be paid out from the trust for a specific period, or life. The Remainder – there's the word – goes to the charity. A charitable Income Trust in a sense is just the opposite. You give the charity income, you don't receive it. What's left (let's avoid the r word) transfers to your heirs or whoever you pick.

My experience with the Charitable Remainder Trust is vastly more extensive than with the Income Trust. It fits right in to dying broke. First, you are assured of annual income. Second, you're entitled to a current-year tax deduction. Third, you can increase the yield on the money if you desire. Fourth, your charity, not the state nor federal government, benefits. There turns out to be an exceedingly attractive additional feature, which I think applies to all charitable giving. No capital-gains tax is due on appreciated assets given to a not-for-profit organization.

Most of us, I think, who live and accumulate much, end up with securities and real estate and shares in a business and collectibles and God knows what else that we acquired when they had little relative value. If we die and leave these assets to others, the cost basis for when those others sell is the value at date of death (or six months later). This so-called stepped-up basis costs the tax man a lot. Basis is just the value you figure future gains and losses from. But this matter really isn't pertinent to dying-poor strategies, is it?

What attracts dying-poor people about charitable giving and tax advantages is that you avoid capital gains taxes but get to take a deduction based on the appreciated value! You reduce not only income tax now but estate tax. What costs the tax man benefits you and those you choose. Even if your purpose is to diversify, charitable trusts can do that by liquidating your highly appreciated securities or real estate tax free.

Sensitive has become a sloppy and debased adjective. If it applies anywhere in this book, it's to the matter of making substantial gifts to friends. Philosophers have faced the puzzle of why gifts so often produce paradoxical effects. Don't let this awareness keep you from taking chances if you give to friends or acquaintances.

Marriages between partners from different backgrounds can be risky. But a little "sensitivity" can turn risk into reward. The common-sense truth is that wealth will always be unevenly and unfairly distributed. Efforts to fix all this have been consistently unsuccessful at the governmental level for centuries. When one person gives to another, what's often missing is sensitivity. Money makes for the most exquisitely private feelings.

On a personal plane you undoubtedly know people whose outlook and way of life would improve mightily if they had more money. It may be a down-on-his-or-her-luck neighbor. A sinking high school or college student. An unfortunate family. An artist or good soul whose labors don't bring in much income. A destitute single parent. A person who needs a medical procedure. We don't have to exhaust my imagination. The "neediest 100,000" are always with us.

I like to think we can recapture the child's way of wondering. "Why doesn't that person just give some money to that other person who needs it so much?" Now's your chance in many cases. Enough moralizing.

I like diplomacy but I like truth more. My belief is that any reader is capable of explaining concisely and consistently why the reader wishes to transfer (weasel word!) some assets to another. The emphasis should be on the donor's decision, the donor's need to do it, the donor's plan to give it away anyway. Correct me if you disagree, but I think the less said about it thereafter the better. Unless the recipient wants to make reports.

I don't know if this observation by Steinbeck isn't exaggerated. He's accurate about the complexity involved. "It is so easy to give, so exquisitely rewarding. Receiving on the other hand, if it be well done, requires a fine balance of self-knowledge and kindness. It requires humility and tact and great understanding of relationships."

Should the beneficiary wish to regard the gift as temporary, as a loan, why not use this old device: Ask the beneficiary to repay the loan to a charity, church, school, whatever, or simply pass the money on to another person who could use it. Your objective is not to get the money. Even the mechanism of "forgivable loan" can come in handy. You "lend" a person say $24,000 for three years and "forgive" $8,000 a year if it's really more of a gift. Certain psychological benefits many times flow from deemphasizing the charitable essence of a gifting arrangement.

Investments

The status quo investment management viewpoint concentrates on the end product. A switch to emphasizing byproducts instead points us toward using asset classes that conventional financial plans play down.

What are these byproducts? Income, of course. Non-preservation of capital becomes newly important. Safety we look at a little differently in the dying-poor mode. Which financial categories are most useful? Things like annuities and reverse mortgages deserve close scrutiny. "Wasting" assets, such as non-renewable natural-resources securities, often work out. GNMAs can behave the same. Even unit trusts eventually "give out," as do mutual funds when the amount withdrawn exceeds the total return.

We drew distinctions on pages 42 and 43 between annuities. You may remember the type useful to providing secure income for the rest of your life. It's clearly a bet between you and the insurance company on when you'll die. They win if you die soon and vice versa. But you've sold them the risk. What you want is guaranteed income to death and/or death of spouse from a longtime triple-A company. As with CDs and mutual funds, there are more than enough places to plunk down your lump sum. Comparison shop among the safe companies. For information on how to obtain company ratings, see pages 43 and 44. A popular variation is the Charitable Gift Annuity. Religious, educational and other charitable organizations offer them. Just ask. In exchange for lifetime income, you donate money. But here there's a twist. You get to deduct a large part of your gift from income tax. Why not all? Because the annuity has a calculable value. Rates aren't usually the highest. The tax advantage, however, is real for most of us. And you are benefiting a worthwhile charity.

Some annuities of this type contain an adjusted-upward payout that tracks inflation. We could use them for a virtually entire dying-poor program. The previous paragraph should be reread if you're ruling out this type of annuity. Naturally, there's a cost. The available base amount of income with an inflation rider starts out lower.

With a mortgage, you make payments to a lender. With a reverse mortgage the lender pays you. When the house is sold, usually by the estate, accounts are settled. This common-sense way of helping finance retirement is typically resisted by financial planners, who typically think uncreatively except on the subject of tax-avoidance. Missing the point, planners reason that other types of borrowing can cost less. Comparison shopping for a reverse mortgage, as with an annuity, is easy these days, however. Lenders now have to furnish plain-spoken disclosure forms. And with long-term reverse mortgages, the kind which dying poor people need, any cost disadvantage over regular borrowing disappears.

Just so you'll be prepared, the Federal National Mortgage Association guidelines allow an up front fee of 1 percent of the residence's value. Closing costs may go to

$2,000 or so. And the big charge is the loan origination fee of up to 2 percent of appraised value. Several thousand dollars total, in other words.

Hinging on life expectancy (you have to be at least 62) and appraised home value, a reverse mortgage can reach 80 percent of built-up equity. The type of deal you desire, should reverse mortgages be needed, is to receive a fixed amount regularly until death. Again the annuity is similar. Because by definition the income from a reverse mortgage is borrowed, it's tax-free. Fees are cranked in. Interest is paid at the finish line.

By accepting an "equity share" agreement with the lending institution, you can squeeze out the highest possible payments. The catch is your estate or heirs give up as much as half of any appreciation that occurs after you take out the reverse mortgage. So what, if dying poor is the objective. Your equity which secures the reverse mortgage otherwise goes into your estate when you die. "Is *that* what you want?" as my assistant used to ask with upraised eyebrows.

A reverse mortgage seems such an odd duck that it's about unclassifiable. By contrast, another important dying-poor tool, the wasting asset, is merely a security, a stock or bond "product."

Government National Mortgage Association (GNMA) issues are pools of home mortgages priced in odd-lot multiples of $25,000. You receive interest and principal each month until the security is used up. You're on the other side of the mortgage equation – receiving interest instead of giving. The principal portion of each check is tax-free, representing the return to you of your own capital.

What's wrong with GNMAs inherently is their sort of counterrotating away from interest-rate trends. What I mean is that when rates are declining, people tend to pay off their mortgages prematurely, returning more money to your GNMA pool faster. Thus you are less locked in when you want to be more locked in. The opposite happens when rates climb. You'd love to get more back faster so you could reinvest at higher rates. But that's precisely the time mortgage borrowers will not prepay. Fortunately, there's enough variety in GNMAs - hugely more than you'd think – so that much of the negative potential can be offset if you're careful.

In a dying-poor scenario, don't let GNMAs be the centerpiece of your spend-it-all strategy. They're a little too unpredictable. But they can be marvelous high-yield AAA parts of the whole.

Natural-resources companies sell the raw material industries work with. Some, like timber, are renewable. More attractive to our point of view here are certain securities of non-renewable suppliers of natural resources. Mines and petroleum head the list.

Any mining company whose existence rests on known deposits can conceivably qualify as a wasting asset. The most convenient examples I'm familiar with are the large numbers of South African gold mines such as Freegold, Vaal Reefs and Western Deep Levels, all owned by Anglo American. Gold Fields of S.A. owns two huge mines, Driefontein and Kloof. In Ghana, Ashanti Gold

Fields has its namesake mines. They can pay good semiannual dividends to shareholders. These not-too-diversified companies may wind up their affairs when their mines are depleted. An American company would branch out more and keep going. The expected number of years left for any of the South African gold companies is relevant available information. And it changes. And changes again.

Dividends from gold mines obviously relate somewhat to the value of gold in the metals markets. Because I have so seldom seen gold work out as an investment, I lead no cheers for this sector. Too, we're in an ultralong-term interest rate downtrend. This undercuts gold's utility as inflation hedge. Precious-metal enthusiasts of course would argue that demand may be growing at a rate of 4 percent and supply at only 3 percent, a large difference. I just wouldn't allocate much of my total assortment of securities to gold issues of any type. Less than 10 percent, to be sure.

The gargantuan petroleum sector has seen the development of hundreds, I'd guess, of ways to invest for various objectives. At this point in history exist many infuriated holders and former holders of "units" of limited petroleum partnerships. To be fair, there are some very satisfied unit holders, too. Unlike vehicles investors are familiar with, these limited partnerships represent, nay, embody, illiquidity. Why? Remember this: There is only one customer for your investment if you want out. Who is that? Your general partner, that's who. There's no "market," in other words.

Let me throw in an observation about illiquidity. Illiquidity can serve an investor's purposes at times. It sounds impossible, I know. The fact is, though, that many of us who call ourselves long-term investors prove too quickly spookable when the unprecedented happens. We can deal with the merely unpredicted. But the unprecedented may make us break our sacred vow to hang on to a security in sickness and in health. The sheer impossibility of selling an illiquid investment many times turns out to be to our eventual advantage.

None of us wants to give up our autonomy, of course, just in case it in time proves "good for us." That's why the popular cross-breed "master limited partnership" came to be. The plan was to retain attractive tax and income benefits of limited partnerships but to add liquidity and diversification. These features of common stock accurately imply what is in fact true: Master limited partnerships from the petroleum industry trade actively in major venues, such as the New York Stock Exchange. They can fit neatly into many portfolios. But no one knowingly designs these entities to be "depleting" assets.

Royalty trusts, however, combine direct ownership of oil and gas in the ground with public markets and dividend payments. Direct ownership of petroleum assets entitles the investor to tax deductions. These come from depletion and expenses and additional special tax credits, such as Section 29. Not surprisingly there are many royalty trusts of all types traded over the counter and (more often) on exchanges. Some larger-capitalization names include BP Prudhoe Bay, San Juan Basin and

Williams Coal Seam. Although nothing actually prohibits these organizations from further development of underlying properties, we are fundamentally putting our money into finite wasting assets. Production of revenue, which largely passes through to us, will cease some time in the future. As this happens the value of the security must decline. Hence its suitability for consideration in a dying-poor financial design.

As I write I can list eight royalty trusts off the top of my head that are paying double-digit returns. Most of the high-paying outfits tend not to feature attractive tax advantages. Some of the other considerations to discuss with your adviser are oil vs. gas, short-lived against long-lived reserves and fully developed or partially developed properties. It will help if the adviser distinguishes between the pure-play survivors of decades past as opposed to more recent creations set up to make the most of Section 29 pass-through credits. As you may suppose, these credits encourage gas development in coal seams, tight sands and other places where extraction poses unusual difficulties.

You may need a trail guide to sort all this out. The appeal nonetheless is real. An investment in a crucial commodity that pays well now, with tax advantages, promises to go out of existence at some foreseeable point, as do we all. The great unknown is just when that will happen.

Mutual funds pay income regularly if you like. That's what bond funds are used for. Equity or stock funds distribute less in income payments but for the most part have better "total" returns, which include appreciation. We therefore have a case for drawing down and eventually exhausting a mutual fund investment through receiving distributions that exceed the investment's overall return.

Let's say you have a good low-risk fund like T. Rowe Price Equity Income or Washington Mutual, where my own 401(k) is. Let's say that for a number of years the average return on your fund has been 14 percent and for the sake of illustration it stays that way for the next decade or two. By taking out 16 percent a year when the fund delivers only 14 percent you could deplete the fund completely over 15 years. A less optimistic but quite realistic example would be a fund with a 9 percent total return. If you wanted to use this fund up over a 10-year period, you would take out 15 percent in your "withdrawal plan." Perhaps needless to say, if the fund's return works out equal to or better than the payout rate, the investment lasts indefinitely. But that wouldn't ordinarily suit dying-poor purposes.

Appendix C is a withdrawal chart. Manipulating the payout, earnings and duration variables can give a pretty likely approximation – no guarantees – of how you can maximize income and principal to you while having the stake last as long as you want it to.

Unlike mutual funds, unit trust managers do not buy and sell securities to achieve best results. Packagers of unit trusts in effect freeze the contents of each trust when it's put together. Most of us think Nuveen or IMIT (Insured Municipal Investment Trust) or something like that when we hear the term. It happens that many unit trusts exist that contain stocks or taxable bonds or odd kinds of things. Let's not go into all that but rather stick to what many of us know: tax-exempt bond portfolios. All bonds mature sooner or later unless they've already been called ahead of time. *Called* means redeemed in advance of maturity by the issuer, incidentally.

A new unit trust may have "call protection" of, oh, 10 years or so on the bonds frozen in the portfolio. After that the capital you've invested starts dribbling back to you until the trust goes away. That may take a dozen years or so. It depends on the "coupon" or stated rate of the bonds and the relation of the coupon to the "interest rate environment." High coupons get called quicker. But secondhand unit trusts come in all stages of depletion. Brokerage houses inventory them, as do the issuers of unit trusts themselves. For our strategy I would ask a registered representative if he or she could assemble some "used" unit trusts that will go out of existence gradually. Each should be expected to terminate at different dates. We call it "laddering" or "staggering" maturities.

If the rep is intellectually unequipped to do this, ask that the firm's unit trust department provide a list with your objectives in mind. Or go elsewhere.

Collateralized Mortgage Obligations also go away in time. As with unit trusts you or someone has to work to assemble a wasting package in line with themes of dying poor. Is it worth it? The more diversification the better, but neither unit trusts nor CMOs make it easy enough for most of us to bother, I imagine. Still, if you like the AAA quality, stable credit (through the years), monthly payment and yield advantages, CMOs can do the job at hand. For dying-poor plans, look for a PAC (planned amortization class). A schedule of principal payments is useful. Avoid "Companion Bonds." They yield more but evidence more volatility in duration of "average life" or length.

Finding the Middle

One of the many fallacies I've been prone to is that of the excluded middle. The "either this way or not at all" kind of thing. To insist on a prerogative may be correct in legal philosophy. To be a purist may result in better, higher art. But sticking to an extreme in financial or investment planning is often to guarantee nothing better than a mediocre outcome. At times the result can approach disaster. The summit of serious planning is compromise: the middle.

In America for the last few decades we've overused military imagery in almost any area of life you can name. "The war on this or that." "I was shot down." "Route 209 is the Ho Chi Minh trail." "It came in under our radar." In my original outline for this chapter I called one Roman numeral heading, "Two asset-management themes at war." Isn't this precisely the wrong way to decide what to do? Later in the outline my senses returned with the sentence, "Plan may be needed to meet both objectives." That's the essence of benefiting from the radical, fresh, somewhat original notion of spending it all before we're gone. Suddenly it's respectable to consider it.

One of the reasons not to go overboard on dying poor is that you flirt with another fallacy: that of "misplaced concreteness." No, this does not mean putting a paved walk on a neighbor's property, as a fellow planning board member joked. It refers to attempting to quantify the unknown (put a number on it) or in our case the unknowable. Specifically our own date of expiration. Death takes, as Auden observed, "the rolling in money." He was referring to how unexpected death can be, taking also "the innocent young" and "the screamingly funny," which rhymes with "rolling in money." Many people may have said what I heard attributed to centenarian Eubie Blake (1883-1983). "If I'd known I was going to live this long I'd have taken better care of myself." A pungent wisecrack by Jeanne Moreau also applies here: "I'm too old to die young." Which reminds me of the rueful remark, "Oh, I've got plenty of money. So long as I die next Thursday."

The practical investment dilemma is that if you diversify – and it's as recommended as regular breathing – you just cannot throw everything into an annuity and hope things work out. By shuffling your asset mix you can arrange to die relatively poor but not exactly broke. Leave dying broke to flat-earthers, know-it-alls and modern-day village explainers. Cut generous slack for the unexpected.

I can't think of any good argument for neglecting ourselves so our heirs will be better off. There's general agreement on this. But there's a not unrelated matter where irrationality is widespread, even the rule it sometimes appears. That is the inability or unwillingness to recognize a rainy day when it hits us. We should give thought in advance on what our attitude will be when serious setbacks strike. My creed is spend freely on ourselves to get us through bad patches. There's a bleak honesty to the question, "What are you saving it for, if not this?" Taking good care of ourselves is a cornerstone of dying poor.

The downshifting movement, neither fast-fading fad nor yet a lasting trend, has a secret in my view. Downshifters simply seize the good things that money is supposed to enable us to buy.

You know, ease, lack of pressure, freedom from free-floating anxiety, plenty of recreation, healthy habits, stress on companionship instead of competition, time, post-materialistic spending habits, individualism. Sounds pretty attractive, albeit a little like the Summer of Love. The point is that you can always do this if it becomes intrinsically attractive. Dying poor neither enhances nor diminishes downshifting. All they may necessarily share is that both are new takes on how to deal with financial success. They fracture long-held ideas and reassemble the pieces into what may someday become dominant middle-class values.

This is an age of remarkable social transformation, to borrow Peter Drucker's phrase. As always, though, it's the individual or family against the system or government. People with independent senses of what's right and wrong in our society work by the rules, even if they're working the rules. But we're interested in the effects on society of a serious attitudinal shift. What might be the unintended consequences of, for example, ending the draft, legalizing drugs, affirmative action, the G.I. Bill, community colleges, all sorts of things. Would replacing estate planning with dying poor in any way weaken or strengthen which strands of society?

People will disagree about it, of course. But I think dying poor enriches family relations by coming down on the side of more communication, more consultation, ultimately more respecting the wishes of others. The effect on the economy would presumably be positive near term because of added consumption. If estate planning is sort of a secret savings program, dropping it would not help the economy longer term. But the newly bared teeth of international capitalism's aggressive side show us that the individual should look first to his or her own personal economy. The larger economy will do quite well for itself, thank you. Just keep in mind that the "larger economy" in the future will be global, not North American.

Sociological speculation can be fun. My viscera tell me that dying poor fosters a more expansive way of life. Cocooning doesn't comport with spending or giving away all your money. Dying poor almost requires that we involve ourselves with the surrounding world.

Figuring out what we really want is to resolve a lot of life's impasses. Deciding whether or not to use up and give away your money may be an impasse for you. Too often we don't follow the sensible path of figuring out what we want and following through on it. Career choices, life partners, places we live – frequently they just happen. In fact most people never *get* to estate planning. Let alone move beyond it.

The advice industry, parasitically, creates anxiety. It has always implied that instead of perhaps a better way, there's the best way. Coyly, the industry stirs up additional insecurity by omitting the critical tools to make ultimate choices. The secret, usually, is that in fact there are no such tools. From *Cosmo* and *Esquire* up to Bill Bennett and Socrates, the best they can tell you is decide for yourself. It has to come from within anyway, don't the dependency groups point out?

Exactly. In our case, estate planning vs. dying poor, neither alternative proves right or wrong. If the dying poor prospect makes you nervous, don't do it. Follow your heart. If giving and spending liberate you from money worries, give and spend.

Talking about how not to exclude the middle, mix a little estate planning and a little charity-self indulgence until you're satisfied. In the advice business one of the surest signs of uncertainty and insecurity on the part of opinion engineers is insistence. Dogma from the priesthoods of planners, brokers, lawyers or trust officers is a danger sign. Tell 'em your karma ran over their dogma.

If you own or will own $1 million you have enough sense to find your path. And don't fear to change your mind later. You yourself may change; circumstances will certainly change. If you've read this far, you're not the kind of person who needs cautioning about how to avoid unthinking comfort zones. Just take with you the knowledge that you can arrive at a happy ending from any number of directions.

* * *

Short answer: Choose between the values of leaving it behind or using it up or a blend of both. Take steps now to cover the bases. Refuse to be buffaloed by financial and legal professionals – there's no "right answer." Follow their advice on specifics and your own for philosophy.

> "... God, or the Great Whoever, has been so lavish in his gifts that you can lose some absolutely priceless ones, the equivalent of whole kingdoms, and still be indecently rich."
> – Wilfred Sheed

Chapter Five

Making It Grow

Preservation of capital sounds nice, like summer afternoon. To many people the term refers to safety. "Preserving" something means keeping it, like a jar of figs. But the way I'm familiar with preservation of capital differs. It has to do with maintaining the value of your assets in a "real" sense. Remember, real means adjusted for inflation. If your return is 9 percent and inflation is 3 percent your real return is only 6 percent.

Inflation, we see, is the evildoer that must be at least neutralized if we preserve capital. In seeking to preserve capital, it almost goes without saying, we hope and intend to outrace inflation. If our investment returns exceed inflation and are not all spent or given away, we "enhance" capital. We make it grow.

Over time, and growth needs time, no-growth approaches chillingly underperform appreciation-focused methods. There's no reason a millionaire can't ordinarily take advantage of a longer time horizon. Let's look at the difference between a 7 percent return, not unusual for a conservative income portfolio, and 13 percent, good but not prizeworthy for growth securities. If 10 years ago you dedicated $500,000 to low or no growth returns averaging 7 percent and took nothing out, today you'd have almost $1 million. (Remember the Rule of 72?) But if $500,000 returned 13 percent the 10-year amount would add an extra $700,000.

For many decades families counted on residential real

estate to provide enormous appreciation not only in nominal but in real terms. That can still occur, but only rarely and never dependably. Consensus views peg residential real estate to rise in value long term up to 2 percent more than inflation. The appreciating part is the land; houses depreciate now. And houses require at least 1 percent of value be spent each year on repairs and maintenance. The older the house, the higher the percentage.

The growth asset of choice now is financial – common stock of the type known as growth stock. Shares in these companies yield almost all of their return through higher per share prices, not dividends. Earnings, instead of being paid out to investors as dividends, are spent by the company on itself. Usually research and development and/or finding and developing new markets take most of the money. If things work out to plan, the company benefits and is worth more as a result.

The wide-awake growth stock investor may properly think of himself or herself as a part owner of the business. Thus it's the long-term outlook that counts most. There are risks in growth investing. Clearly the bird is in the bush, not the hand. That comes later, when you sell at a profit. Many growth investments sell at a loss, of course. It's thus even more essential in growth investing to be fully diversified than in cases of supersafe but lower potential portfolios.

Let's not forget the tax slant. Long-term capital-gains tax rates tend to remain lower than income tax rates for high-income people. But that's only if you sell, and you may not sell. It's more efficient, too, for the company to use earnings internally than for you to have to pay the ordinary income tax rate on dividend income (taxed twice, in other words). You retain some tax control with growth securities that has pretty much vanished elsewhere.

You probably aren't reading this book to learn how to pick stocks. Or mutual funds specializing in growth stocks. There do exist some widely accepted principles, nonetheless, that it's usually best not to flout too often.

Strong financial positions come first in my book. Rule of thumb, it's preferable that a company not owe more than half its own value. Growth companies borrow so much that the favorable terms strong companies are granted mean a lot when they do borrow.

Volume or sales should show consistent up trends. If the Gross Domestic Product (GDP) grows by x, our company's sales should be x plus something. In today's low-inflation setting, sales gains through price increases are in many cases ancient history. Real growth, or "unit" growth, attracts investors. Remember, you need people to buy the stock after you buy it and to be willing to pay more than you did.

Valuation usually involves a company's price/earnings ratio. Sometimes we call this a P/E or a multiple. Most of the time we compare a growth company's P/E to that of the average stock, which may be, say 18. A hot, exciting stock may have a very high P/E (the preferred cliche is astronomical, with unsustainable trailing close behind). For the non-speculative investor it's usually best not to buy shares at a P/E above the company's predicted growth rate. Look at the year-ahead earnings growth guesstimate. If it's 20 percent don't pay more than 20 times earnings. Lower is even better.

Growth portfolios should shun cyclicals. The challenges are different and the growth discipline doesn't work well. The economy drives cyclicals. What are they? Autos, airlines, entertainment (not everyone agrees), paper, chemicals, steel, copper, cement, machine tools, newspapers, aerospace, restaurants (again, in my opinion).

Can I just buy a growth mutual fund and forget about it? You can indeed succeed with a good fund. Remember, though, that the fund manager gets paid to buy and sell. Recall also that when people panic and redeem mutual fund shares the manager has to sell during a panic – the worst time. Buying and selling may improve a fund's performance. It should. But it gives up a primary benefit to wealthy investors: long-term tax-deferred stock holding. Also surrendered is the tailoring of a portfolio just for you. Even the best mutual funds are off-the-rack solutions fitting *you* in. For the affluent, fitting *investments* in makes for more personalized results.

To set up a portfolio of individual growth stocks, let's refresh our memories from Investing 101 as to guidelines.

The benefits of diversification can be obtained with eight-or-10 stocks. There's no real point in owning more than 20. Ideally, don't bother with a stock that's less than 5 percent of the total value. Otherwise it won't matter too much what happens to it. But more than 15 percent in one stock can put a portfolio at an unnecessary risk. And don't bunch up more than 25 percent in any single industry. Certainly no more than 35 percent in even a large macrosector, such as non-cyclicals or finance. In a stretch, these rules can work for an entire total-return portfolio as it happens.

Applying common sense and cooling one's adrenaline jets will let us use the foregoing commandments to build our own platform. Maybe it sounds too much like jargon. But to me a growth platform has two parts. First you form a plan of action, reflecting any pertinent personal values. Then you put it into effect. On a larger scale, (let me just squeeze this in,) someone has to do something similar with all your assets as a whole.

"Just what I need, another job," an assistant remarked when recycling was mandated. No matter how you feel about managing your investments, and this person had nothing against recycling, life for many of us is already too complicated. The very idea of holding ourselves responsible for "growing" the family assets sounds too much like going back to school. And definitely not the school of lawn tennis and the Loire Valley. Rather, the school of grubby work and non-stop reading and constant fear of failing. Fixed-income investing may allow for periods of relative passivity if not exactly tranquility. Growth investing does not.

Money Managers

The investment-management industry in the industrial world thus flourishes. Don't think of yourself as copping out if you'd rather have someone do the work for you. I think it's a perfectly sensible way to free up more time for things you do like. And it's logical that the right professional should know a great deal more than most clients and wield that knowledge with less negative emotion. My personal preference is for money managers to proceed hand in hand with investors. Both continue learning from each other on this not uninteresting journey. A very large percentage of the wealthy, it must be said, just want to delegate the work of watching investments.

Checklists aren't the warmest technique for exploring possible relationships. In the absence of an unqualified referral from our most respected acquaintance, however, we have to survey a number of criteria.

If you weren't sent to the manager or company by someone, does the individual or organization have references and endorsements you or perhaps your lawyer can follow up? You're searching for good experiences with clients you can identify with.

How does the organization rank as to character and reputation? And the management? You want evidence of quality and commitment. Sooner or later, you'll probably have to rely on your adviser's judgment. And not just on investments. The organization must have enough depth and experience to counsel you on any financial terrain. So, do you like them? Are they committed? Can you trust them?

An organization or key individual must spell out investments policies and viewpoints fairly precisely.

There should be a consistency that produces superior results. Compensation of the people you would work with, in my opinion, should depend to some extent on their effectiveness and productivity. The tradition of long, lazy client lunches, to cite a convenient example, should be replaced in most areas of asset management by a professional work ethic of delivering real value to clients. In alignment with incentive pay for professionals, you may wish to inquire about performance-based management fees. There are a few pure money-management firms that offer this late-blooming innovation. If you're lucky enough to know an individual who manages portfolios, that's worth a try, once you've verified good references, philosophies and investment results. From experience, I can tell you that clients of individual managers tend to be the happiest.

Some market efficiency is visiting the investment advisory world. Middle-six- or -seven-figure accounts usually end up paying 2 percent of asset value a year when fees and transactions are added up. There are some 1 percent and 3 percent exceptions. If you're paying a 3 percent wrap fee, commissions and management combined, ask for 2 percent. You'll get it. Don't forget that as assets rise, so do adviser's cuts. And vice versa.

Speculation

Speculation is on the wilder shore of growth investing, I concede. It does aim, as growth investing can, to buy and sell for a quick profit, nothing more. But hunting isn't homicide, and speculation isn't growth investing. Real speculation is gambling. I think people who associate speculation with securities markets are like people who first think of placing bets when they think of professional sports.

Are pro sports so boring that to make them interesting money bets have to be placed? As a non-gambler, all I know is that sports per se, boring as they usually are, have to be about something worthwhile. And that thing is not wagering. Gambling piggybacks on sports; speculation piggybacks on the securities markets.

But it's a free country. Speculation is consenting economic behavior between adults. And that's the spirit in which it belongs. Do it if it's fun. If you think you're the kind of social and economic visionary who was thinking Internet when everybody else was thinking cable.

The fool's gold rule is never to speculate with more than 5 percent of your financial capital. That can still turn out to mean a lot of risk taking, especially when you recall that differing risks are already part of everything you own, including a savings account. Even though you may use your regular account to speculate, take care to segregate gambling from investing in your and your broker's mind. I'm not holier than thou, and I disagree entirely with moralists who call speculation a narcotic. I'm more like the ocean-racing yacht owner's wife, Patricia Buckley, who compared the sport to standing in an icy shower tearing up $1,000 bills. Too, there's a dangerous escalator effect in any ultraexpensive hobby. "The next level is better," choruses your new set of peers. Sometimes, as someone said of polo, speculation becomes a disease. And the only cure is poverty.

Tax Advantages

These years are very uncertain periods to write about taxes. There are at least three contending philosophical currents besides what all the commentary covers. The first is, and it's kind of a caveat, "Watch what they do, not what they say." If we have a bipartisan elite, they share a language that has meaning apart from what the words and sentences say. But the membership understand each other. I remember how the Tax Equity and Fiscal Responsibility Act cake was baked while Treasury and White House officials agreed with Senate and House Finance and Ways and Means committee spokesmen who appeared to despair of compromise. Tax loopholes vaporized soon after, catching us and many lobbyists off guard. That was in 1986.

The second deep current may always ultimately defeat permanent improvements in tax code crafting. The secret promise of unpredictable tax policy is power to the legislators' re-election field marshals. (Block that military metaphor!) Even if we move to a simple, understandable system like the flat tax, those interests who see themselves as specifically not privileged by the new order will flood key congressmen with desirable cash. The nibbling away will start all over and continue until the new system is flayed. It wasn't long after 1986 when the pledge not to monkey with tax brackets was violated. If we were to violate precedent, develop a fair tax system and stick with it, how long do you think big campaign checks from special interests would continue?

One other way of thinking, the third of these currents, holds out more promise. Faintly. It is the swallowing by much of the public and media of the originally bone-headed notion that deficits are bad. Deficits don't matter that much and ours aren't nearly as bad in context as people say. Most people who even use the term really mean national debt, $3 trillion, the result of all past deficits. This debt consists of the Treasury securities investors and Social Security and savers depend on. They're a good thing, not a bad thing.

But I won't argue with people who disagree. Just as deficits don't really matter, a lot of people thinking they do doesn't cause any harm either. What is important, and it's supremely important, is that the rate of growth of deficits point in the right direction – down. It's really wonderful if the deficits themselves go down in real or even nominal numbers. Then we're on track. The 1995 deficit was lower than in 1982, when the Dow-Jones Industrials, now 5,000 plus, were under 1,000. This is one of those many instances where the journey signifies and the destination doesn't.

So general tax policy and attitudes matter. To business, they matter more than who's in power. Twenty years ago who could have predicted that a conservative like Reagan would let deficits metastasize? Or that a liberal like Clinton would make deficit limits a centerpiece of his reign? Republicans use deficit phobia to starve liberal programs. Democrats profess concern over the deficit debt to prove they're really more conservative than they seem.

Just as economies have always overpowered countries, economic attitudes dominate Congress and administrations. Not the other way around. But none of this tectonic shifting is in reach of readers. The question down at our level is how growth investing works to limit taxes legally and intelligently. We think of millionaires as paying much higher rates than the less favored. But being a millionaire lets you direct investments and cash flows without worrying about how to get through the next month. Most people are prisoners of the tax system: It nails the consumer. Readers can at least get out on parole.

Capital Gains

Capital-gains taxes in my experience are one unusual feature of the United States revenue system. Not only are they seldom found elsewhere, our states also impose these levies. States, remember, will begin to receive relatively less money from Washington in the next while. State taxes will take unexpected twists to recoup "lost" federal checks. Regardless, capital gains taxes being lower than income taxes, prudent people often boost in-pocket returns by emphasizing growth programs. The longer you let gains pile up without selling, the longer the company where you're part owner (shareholder) has use of your money. If the company pays earnings out in dividends, you will receive only 65 cents after they pay the top corporate rate of 35 percent.

And when you finally do sell, not to be repetitive, the

gains rate will prove less than the marginal income tax bracket on your income. And, if you never sell, your heir will not have to pay capital gains. Neither will a non-profit group, like a church or college, if you give or leave them stock which has appreciated.

Before we move on, let's make sure, as they say in Washington, that we're on the same page. Are we all agreed that, attractive as capital-gains tax strategies can be, minimizing taxes should remain a secondary objective? Tax factors must not dominate investment decision making. But always weigh them when choosing stocks, holding stocks and selling stocks.

Reinvested Earnings

At this point in history, people wonder how much things will change regarding after-tax returns if radical tax proposals ever triumph. Will capital-gains positioning even matter? Actually not, if either the consumption (sales or value added) levy or the flat tax took over. But they're not going to triumph, as we discussed, except in a highly hedged and modified form. Washington surrender the power to tinker? Not in this life. For the record, both sales and flat taxes would return about the same percentage to investors. Between the two, what I've read of the sales tax sounds superior. It would alas be impossible to implement. Too many unanswerable-in-advance complexities.

Zero-Coupon Municipals

Remember when bonds used to have coupons? Owners would scissor off those little rectangles to turn in for money every six months. In the investment business we retain the term *coupon* to signify how much money a bond pays. The coupon is 6 percent, say. If a bond did not pay income but grew in value instead, it wouldn't have a coupon, would it? Hence "zero coupon" means in effect growth bond. And if the zero is a municipal instrument, it's another tax-advantaged growth instrument. The way zeros work is you buy a $1,000 bond at a discount, perhaps a few hundred dollars depending on yield and maturity. At maturity you receive $1,000. Or if you sold it before maturity you receive market value, generally a reflection of how much interest has been accruing during the time you held the bond added to the price you paid when buying it. Bond values fluctuate in the market until the bonds mature. Zeros more than most.

Many points favor tax-free zero-coupon bonds. Compounding, or interest on interest, remains a pleasantly surprising plus for bond buyers. Reinvestment is efficient. And not only do you not have to plow back odd amounts of money (the semiannual payment), one rate of interest is assured during the life of the bond on the principal and reinvested interest. Normally, if you think about it, bond interest available sinks lower as years to maturity decline. Because reinvested interest will have shorter and shorter maturities as time advances, returns obtained will decline accordingly. Not so with a zero. At date of purchase the rate is set all the way to maturity, just like any other bond. And, importantly, you know the date when the payback is certain.

Why isn't this the perfect growth investment then? It's a return problem. Even though tax-exempt bonds are anomalously paying 90 percent as much as taxable Treasuries, after-tax comparisons over a five-, 10- or 15-year period with growth stocks would put the stocks at a two-or-three-times higher total return. But zero munis do offer an awfully convenient, awfully good return for the amount of safety they bring. In high-tax states, sprinkle a growth portfolio with a few percent of these if you have no objection to veering a little off the equity path.

Annuities

For growth, the variable annuity has real advantages. Consisting of a no-load mutual fund inside a tax-deferred package, the variable product can have death benefits too. A feature sometimes found is the insuring of the value of your investments, notched up annually to keep pace with your fund's performance. But this is a death benefit only.

Let's refresh our memories of the tedious labyrinth of insurance industry gizmos. The tax-deferred package resembles a non-deductible IRA with no limit on the size of investment. As with an IRA, you have to be 59 1/2 years old to make penalty-free withdrawals. But unlike an IRA, you do not have to begin withdrawals at 70 1/2. Why does this prosthetic device part of the investment body even exist? The potency of the insurance lobby is the sole conceivable reason. And, as with IRA's, 401(k)s and such, you pay ordinary income tax on money pulled out of a variable annuity at that time.

But thank heaven for small favors. This is another

way to achieve tax-advantaged growth that's legal and even on the conservative side. Rule of thumb, look for costs to settle out at about 2 percent a year vs. a comparable mutual fund-only net of perhaps 1 percent. There's a lot of difference in performance among the many mutual fund choices in variable annuities. Make your adviser work to justify his recommendations. Something better may lie around the corner. If doing this yourself without an adviser, use a systematic approach to compare performance, at least in your rear-view mirror.

Page 43 of *What To Do With A Million Dollars* shows how to check up on insurance company strength. Stick with the strong, of course. The extreme regard for safety we would show if this were the provider chosen for an immediate life annuity can be played down slightly if there's good enough reason. You're usually not handing over your future to a variable annuity.

Asset Allocation

Asset allocation has become such a pop cure-all in "financial" journalism that I wish we had a fresh term. The real difficulty anyway for most people is risk allocation. Do I understand and wish to take on the offsetting risks built into a diversified (allocated) normal investment program? Before we try to strip some of the fear away from everyday risks, like that of missing the boat, let me run through the high points of diversification. With insectlike monotony, articles try first to scare us that we can't afford college for our kids, can't afford to retire, can't afford comfortable lives, unless we – magic-phrase

– asset allocate. You have to forgive me because the subsequent Chicken Little formulas for salvation (second part of same article) jump out at me at least once a week, it seems.

All individual investing fits into one -or-more of the following: aggressive growth, growth, balanced, conservative or risk-averse. Aggressive-growth portfolios mostly consist of stocks with a little cash. Opposite that is risk-averse with everything in bonds and cash except for a little common stock. Stocks, going back as far as we have data, outperform bonds more than 2-to-1. As we move across the spectrum, the higher the percentage of stocks, the higher the volatility in any given year. And the higher the performance over various holding periods. Aggressive growth as a category for five- or 10-year periods may average in the low- to midteens as to total return. Risk-averse during the same sample periods runs in the middle single figures. Balanced, as you'd expect, performs between these extremes.

The aggressive-growth approach seeks to maximize long-term return. This comes at the expense of a high degree of fluctuation in value measured in given years. Growth emphasizes stock too, but stirs in a little bit of bonds. Ah, there's our term: asset mix! Growth stresses future appreciation as well and puts income growth ahead of current income. As with aggressive growth, year-to-year predictability of principal is played down in importance.

Balanced means stocks, bonds and plenty of cash. Current income, future appreciation and growth of income are given approximately equal importance. Conservative stacks up likewise but with a lot less stock. Appreciation and growth of income are just secondary objectives. Risk-averse has only a relatively token stock position. It seeks to protect stability of principal while extracting maximum income.

I don't recall the general outlines of asset mixing having changed much over recent years. But there is one major change affecting everyone. And there are a couple of deviations from the norm that apply more to the rich.

The major change is the shift in advice for most people to weight their investments more to common stocks than before. One obvious reason is that longevity requires better performance. At the same time longevity allows longer holding periods and thus wider swings in price (short-term volatility). Too, we've all been constrained to note how employers are dumping responsibility for managing our retirement assets back on us. Previously, professional retirement-plan asset managers would have banked more on stocks than feels reasonable to the average worker. Thus, the advice industry thinks, ordinary folk must be educated to trust that equities (stock) do work out a lot better in the long run. The practical effect is that an adviser who counseled only 25 percent or 30 percent stock in a conservative portfolio a few years ago may now have jacked that up to 35 percent or 40 percent or even more now. This is just a hypothetical example, but close enough.

For the rich, asset managers try to achieve performance rates that mandate growth levels of return over time. Too-heavy a concentration in bonds undermines appreciation. Thus we see surprisingly small bond positions in contemporary account statements of the rich.

The other item pertaining to the rich no less than the rest of us is the human tendency to spend all the income we earn. Expenditures rise to meet the income available, or something like that – kind of a modified Parkinson's Law. Asset managers of the rich themselves set an example by tilting asset mixes strongly toward stock, with its lower income yield. Capital preservation and enhancement thus come first. In these cases there's still plenty of income and growth of income in an absolute sense.

All of us know people in their 80s who probably never expected to end up there. Their expectations developed in their youth. At that time the knowledge available predicted that only a few would survive much beyond retirement age. And that only a very few, instead of what we now know to be a great many, would live to be 90 or more. The "old old" in fact are now creating a new stage of human existence.

Similarly we, like the old old in their younger or middle years, base our hopes and investment goals on what seems most reasonable now. Today. When we look back, decades hence, we may find that we were shortsighted. Most of us may face a greater need for growth, for preservation and enhancement of capital, than we realize today.

The same extension of average life spans that makes us apprehensive about having enough money throughout all our remaining years in fact contains the means for arranging that we indeed do. It is the higher returns that growth investing delivers. It is the ability to invest long term that lets us absorb the short-term risks that attend growth investing. And it is the need, almost the demand, to invest long term that provides the incentive. We are longer term as people. So should our investments be.

Depending on the period of time or number of years covered, calculations are made and published about the performance of all the asset classes. We've referred to it and we all have been exposed to this information in media and in prospectuses and promotional pieces. Except for the major indices the figures bounce around a bit. Usually the variations serve the purposes of something being sold or some point being made. The details don't matter. But one consistent motif does. This motif is that growth assets – total return or growth stocks – are close to three times as productive as very conservative securities. They return more than twice as much as other non-growth investments. The difference in impact over 10-or-15 years is jolting.

Use growth stocks to accomplish the appreciation part of your objectives. Even non-growth equities tend to rise in value over the years. This proves especially so if dividends go up periodically. The old rule was to subtract your age from 100 to derive your appropriate percentage of stocks. If you are 55, you should keep 45 percent in equities. The new rule, in my view, is to keep as high a proportion in stock, particularly in growth and total-return companies, as your risk profile and your present income needs allow. Kierkegaard observed that though life can be only understood backward, it must be conducted forward. The same with investing. Growth securities worked in the past. Use them now and in the future.

* * *

Short answer: Unless you are certain you have all the money you will need (even the richest rarely think this), focus on growth as a cornerstone of any investment program not devoted solely to present-day safety or income.

Chapter Six

Giving Part Away

Two chapters back in "Should I die broke?" the question of giving assets away played a prominent part. The more mainstream tack which Chapter Six now takes deals with explicit ground rules. It is carefully researched and as up to the minute as publication schedules allow. But I must stress that tax and legal professionals, to which groups I don't belong, must approve and in most cases help implement the methods covered.

Gifting targets either people or charities. We assume it's irrevocable. Tax advantages abound. Usually they involve current-income deductions and estate-tax lessening. Continuing income streams to the donor from the very donated assets themselves can expand, believe it or not, when we apply specific gifting devices and techniques. These remain the principal financial motivators. Although the percentage of federal revenue raised by gift and estate taxes proves quite tiny – about 1.3 percent of the total – the prospect of paying them makes millionaires employ complex maneuvers to avoid doing so. I'll try to steer around the chokingly dense rules and regulations to concentrate instead on the useful things. My aim is to give you enough information to point toward the tools sophisticated asset owners (and others) use to leverage their accumulated wealth. Even if they have to get rid of it to do so.

Gifting Ground Rules and Taxes

When mulling over gifting possibilities, keep in mind a couple of tax principles. They usually apply. One is that tax law lets us deduct amounts contributed to charity. If it's cash or property, which includes securities, itemize the amounts on your return. Use fair market value. On anything substantial, make sure a lawyer or accountant scans the donation for any limits. Restrictions can crop up. They have to do with the nature of the gift, the type of charity, and the way the gift is used. In fact, though, most people, I think, encounter no material barriers most of the time. Even a partial deduction is usually large.

This income tax deduction, regrettably, doesn't apply to gifts to individuals. But your exposure to estate taxes diminishes when you transfer assets to others. Without even having to report it, we can give $10,000 away to anyone in a given year. Mr. and Mrs. Smith can give each of their two children $20,000 and each of their four grandchildren $20,000. Within the scope of a typical family, $100,000 goes out this way each year. And they as a couple can give each of their children's spouses $20,000 additionally. Pretty soon this adds up. Anyone can give up to $10,000 to anyone yearly with no reporting or tax consequences. People who have received gifts can give them back. That's legal too.

Not to complicate the austere simplicity of the $10,000 gift, but there's the $600,000 gift or estate exclusion as well. Not only can you leave an untaxed estate amount of $600,000 when you die, you can give that much away during your life. You just can't do both. You can combine gifts and inheritances up to $600,000 tax free, of course.

Charitable gift annuities, trusts and foundations offer somewhat differing benefits to asset donors. Because charity is involved, decisions often rest on less slit-eyed financial calculations than do investments.

Charitable Gift Annuities

First, let's check out the gift annuity (CGA). As mentioned in Chapter Four, page XX, these agreements let you retain income during your life from contributions made now. Obviously, contributions as such no longer belong to you. Therefore your taxable estate, if there is one, will amount to less. That's good. Additionally, however, you receive a valuable income tax deduction now. The present value of the future benefit from the gift is deductible. It's a considerable plus, perhaps half, more or less of the properties transferred.

Who provides gift annuities? Religions, organizations, colleges and universities, charities, such as the United Way or the Salvation Army. Who backs the arrangement? The charity's assets.

When does the income start? Whenever you say; usually now. If you defer receiving payments, of course, they will be larger when they start, the charity having had the use of your money. How long does the income continue? Until you die, or until your spouse dies, if you've established that at the outset.

Besides the estate tax advantage, the income tax deduction and the income for life, do other meaningful good points exist? Yes. The first is that you can increase your income stream from the asset. If it has appreciated vs. the income it pays, you can give it to your alma mater and receive let's say 6 percent instead of what may have been 2 percent or 3 percent or less, as one example. No capital-gains tax is due when the charity liquidates your appreciated asset. Another major plus. You've donated the whole thing. Your income derives from the untaxed amount.

And the income that you get is partly a return of capital and in many cases includes a portion that represents long-term capital gains. The tax you pay on this income is thus less that it would have been.

What are the disadvantages of charitable gift annuities? For one the rates offered by the major charities aren't exactly high, and they tend to cluster tightly. Not that these rates are low, but some charities offer rates much higher than most. And all the principal left goes to the charity. For most of us, though, this isn't very disturbing. It's certainly simpler than setting up a charitable trust yourself.

Charitable Trusts

Do you remember the saying, "nothing is valued that is easily obtained?" Does that imply that the more difficult something is, the more valuable? I doubt it. But the series of unavoidable steps it takes to accomplish a charitable trust can produce surprising advantages.

The big motivator often is that you can avoid capital-gains taxes on the sale of assets no matter how low their cost basis. The right kind of trust can use the proceeds to magnify current or future income. The donation itself is deductible, thus lowering income taxes. Done properly, the right kind of trusts will transfer more assets to the family in cases where that's desired.

Your assets are diversified. Your life is simplified. And you've made a real contribution the way you wish.

Charitable Lead Trusts

I think the least common type of charitable trust, though I don't know this, is the lead trust. Think income to the *charity* and remainder to the heirs, not the more common other way around. Interest income "leads" the trust.

If you and your family don't need the income an asset generates, consider the lead trust. You can transfer the asset to your heirs with improved tax implications. The trust may be established while you're alive or put on ice until needed to reduce an estate's gift or estate tax liability. I read somewhere that Mrs. Onassis used this device.

You can choose a guaranteed annuity if you wish. The charity then receives annuity payments. Or you can use what's called a unitrust. This way the value of the assets each year is docked a fixed-percentage of market value at the time.

We have to beware a couple of tax non-advantages with a lead trust. When it's established you do not, and this is important, entitle yourself to an income tax deduction. Income from the donated assets, however, is reported by the trust. It gets a charitable deduction for any income paid out to the charity. Clear as mud?

If you've still maintained more than a shred of interest in hearing additional details of the lead trust, here's the other tax non-advantage. Appreciated assets handed over to a lead trust incur no protection per se from capital-gains tax. The only way to deal with this difficulty is to have the lead trust set up after your death. That way the assets will be stepped up in cost basis to whatever they're worth at death, not when they were acquired.

You can elect the termination date of the trust. That's when assets previously transferred by you or your estate to the trust will be distributed to your heirs. You can also see to it, if you prefer, that the assets go out to heirs in installments. The purpose in doing so is to reduce estate tax liabilities.

There's nothing wrong with charitable lead trusts for wealthy individuals who don't need present income but wish for heirs to inherit assets in question. Income benefits the charity and is removed from the "grantor's" estate, which is preserved for the beneficiaries.

Let's take a breather while I apologize for the word jungle that describing trusts seems to foster. In the appendix is a chart where you can see how your situation comports with what's available.

Just the names themselves are repellent. The clumsiest has to be Qualified Terminable Interest Trust, but at least it's a cute acronym (QTIP). The important trust I must now spend a couple of pages on is the charitable remainder, so let's just flush its graceless name and use CRT.

Charitable Remainder Trusts

This remarkably helpful tool is named for the other part of an asset besides the income. That other part is the "remainder" when a CRT's term winds up. The charity has the right to the property remaining.

A CRT can open the door to any number of advantages that aren't easy to find in one spot anymore, if at all. Avoiding gains taxes, boosting income, cutting current income tax, passing more wealth to the family after death, diversifying assets, simplifying life and doing good deeds have all been mentioned earlier but bear bringing up again. Remember our looking at the CRT from the dying-poor viewpoint in Chapter Four?

Besides all these reasons for establishing a CRT, people have mentioned still others to me. Such other things as preserving profits and gains and protecting an estate from creditors come up now and then.

When CRTs work best, people own highly appreciated assets and want additional income. A six-figure minimum, though in no way required, can justify the several-thousand-dollar legal and other fees that accumulate. There has to be a trustee to file annual tax returns, comply with laws and regulations, handle investments, and so on. Unless you do it yourself, these administrative services cost. Unless you're a lawyer legal bills will have to be paid. An individual, the grantor, serving as trustee, runs a greater risk of audit and compliance rough spots. How well can an individual keep a trust qualified and routinely avoid taxes and penalties?

Charities themselves often act as trustees. Usually

compliance, legal and audit questions are thus minimized or even eliminated. The problem is you can't retain even partial control. You can't switch the charity. You can't change the trustee. And you may disapprove of investment practices to no avail.

I always suggest a corporate trustee. It's easier in many ways and you may change the charity, change the trustee and retain partial control. Professionals of course should reduce the risk of compliance, audit and legal questions. They have investment skills as well.

Remember that the charity takes the principal of the trust when it terminates, not before. For that reason, the "present value" – it's a percentage of the future gift – is tax deductible. Your age is a factor in the formula, as are IRS tables, the specified duration of the CRT and the current interest rate. Higher income draws by you are associated in general with smaller deductions.

Once the amount of your tax deduction is determined you can apply as much as 50 percent of your adjusted gross income if you donated cash. For appreciated securities its 30 percent. But you have carry-forward potential for five years until using up the deduction.

That's for income tax. Similarly, for estate tax, all trust assets usually avoid estate and gift taxes. Your estate obtains an estate-tax charitable deduction when the CRT transfers property.

What about taking out your income, which may jump considerably through repositioning? A low-producing farm, property, or portfolio sold with no capital gains tax can go straight into good income securities.

You can select either a fixed income or a variable. For fixed, we employ a Charitable Remainder Annuity Trust (CRAT). It just gets worse, doesn't it? For variable income it's a unitrust (CRUT). Worse yet.

If you go with fixed, it stays the same for the trust's life. It's like the other side of fixed vs. variable mortgages. The unitrust hedges against inflation because the agreed-upon percentages of assets to be paid out is calculated annually on the changing market value of the principal. The income can go down of course.

Another matter exists to consider between fixed and variable. A CRAT (fixed) can't be added to. You could create another trust, however.

When donating to a CRAT or CRUT, if a capital gain is sheltered, the income to you will surely be taxed annually. If non-appreciated assets or cash fund the trust, income flows to you without capital-gains tax. It is otherwise taxable, but tax-exempt bonds can be used in the vehicle.

One CRUT refinement useful for retirement planning is the "income-only" unitrust. You choose a higher percentage payout than the CRUT can earn at first. Thus you create a deficit account: money "owed" to you. The trustee makes up the deficits when income runs high. So what? Well, just like retirement planning outside a trust, you invest more in growth when you're working and more in income when you're not.

Think of it this way. Say you're making maximum contributions to your retirement plan already. In addition you may establish an income-only CRUT. Make deductible annual contributions that grow while you work.

The last type of CRT to explore is the pooled-income fund. Public charities may invest together the assets of different donors. Income is tied to performance. It's taxable to you. Like a CRUT, the pooled-income fund offers many advantages. The huge disadvantages is lack of input by you, the grantor. No choice of payout, no say on trustees, no changes of beneficiaries.

It is simple, if one-size-fits-all. You don't have to get someone to draft your own document. The pooled-income fund is a product, but real pluses come with the minuses.

Charitable Foundations

Foundations, or charitable foundations, to me used to belong in an advanced estate-planning category, which I touch on in the next chapter. Today they are becoming more common. Not trusts in the ordinary meaning, they can meet philanthropic objectives. Charitable foundations help with taxes, not surprisingly. But it is widely believed to take $250,000 or so to fund an effective foundation.

Private foundations or family foundations are often the lasting means for relatives to make gifts. People sometimes put the family name on their foundation. Besides becoming a source of pride, the foundation can serve as a forum for discussion of family aspirations. Members of a family may become employees of the foundation, taking care to avoid self dealing and unreasonable compensation.

Public foundations, unlike private or family ones, result from the efforts of an organization. Donors use the public foundation as a vehicle. Who benefits? Perhaps a charity designated by the donor or by the foundation.

Some foundations use the "trust" organizational form with trustees. Others are corporations with directors. Certain states prefer one format to another. Your own goals make the final determinations.

As to income from the foundation, you can pretty much not count on it. Foundations must use capital and income solely for their own purposes. Though donors receive no income they can obtain a 100 percent deduction as a tax advantage. Remember that CRTs, gift annuities and pooled-income funds don't permit this.

An important detail is that since Dec. 31, 1994, deductions for contributions to private foundations will be limited to the cost basis on appreciated securities. Public foundations, by contrast, allow for a market-value deduction on donations of appreciated securities.

So far in this chapter, any mention of one item of great concern to many has gone neglected. Except for fans of dying broke, people naturally wonder about what they'll leave behind. Won't charity get it all? Isn't that the catch with heavy-duty charitable stuff?

Replacing Gifted Wealth

A couple of solutions often prove doable. Whether or not it's right for you, everyone should know the priceless gimmick of the "wealth-replacement trust." The more professional moniker is irrevocable life insurance trust or ILIT.

At death, insurance policies are routinely included in the calculation of estate value. Even though yes, the beneficiaries do receive the payoff tax-free and early, the value of the policy bulks up the estate's worth for figuring probate and estate tax. Bummer, as my children used to say. Another trap laid by our tax system for the unwary, which is most of us.

How to outfox them? Don't "own" policies when you die. The owner is defined as whoever names the beneficiaries. That's where the ILIT comes to the rescue. Create a trust just to own policies and pay premiums. Proceeds at death go into the trust and not the estate. The people you want to receive your inheritance are paid off tax free. As you see, this could save a lot in estate taxes and probate costs.

Your checks to the trust for premium payments can count as tax-free up to $10,000 a year. A Mr. Crummey sued successfully for this right in the 1960s. Almost as if in retaliation, the government requires you to notify beneficiaries each year that they can withdraw your payments for their own use. No wonder there's so much hypertension in America! But don't neglect these "Crummey notices" or the gifts become subject to tax.

The final assets to which heirs take possession will generally far exceed in value that which would have been left after estate taxes. At least with an estate of some heft. Remember, a separate trust must be established to own the policy. And don't forget that one way to fund it could be contributing tax savings or additional income resulting from the charitable gift. It's not always enough, but it helps.

At this point, were I the reader and you the writer, I would think, "There's the catch! Aha! What if they don't approve me for life Insurance? I've already had a pre-Hillary hassle with my employer about medical coverage. Forget life!" Actually, as we may know from experience, life insurance companies do want to issue coverage. That's their function. But many of us will remain virtually uninsurable. How can our children benefit?

The answer is that a payment provision for children should go into the CRT at the time you set it up. The clause in question mandates that the trust endure beyond the demise of parents for a specified number of years. It's called a "term-of-years trust payment schedule." In effect, this stipulation serves to replace the life policy that would have replaced the wealth. Either way, the kids are fine. It just takes longer.

You can see to it that the final structure of the trust establishes the payout rate you want. You determine how flexible it should be, what are the provisions for charity and what, if any, are the provisions for *heirs*.

Eventually, the professionals stitching all the trust remnants together will ask you who should administer the trust. Needed in the future will be annual evaluations, tax computing, accounting and distributions. Someone must prepare tax and information returns. The operation of the trust requires the maintenance of records.

You can sense the problem here of a donor serving as trustee and trying to administer the CRT as well. Never do it. Mistakes can disqualify a trust.

In fact, don't even be the trustee. The facts make a clear-cut case for corporate trustees. A trust company or bank can see that the assets are managed according to directives. All paperwork becomes their responsibility. Records, distributions and ultimate dissolution of the trust are trust companies' stock in trade.

In case you're interested, and I am, both state and federal agencies regulate corporate trustees. Courts think of them as experts and expect higher performance.

Corporate trustees remain objective and reliable, unlike many individuals with their personal ups and downs. If you want to control, say, investment choices, act as a co-trustee. Don't count on friends or family.

By the way, you retain the power to replace corporate trustees. Happily their fees come out of the trust assets, not your income stream. These are the assets going to the charity anyway. It's not even your money anymore.

Divorce

People who've passed through the valley of death divorce-style may not find "Giving Part Away" an appropriate chapter to cover the subject. Actually, *cover* is way too big a word for this short treatment.

Statistically all married couples run some risk of permanent breakup. This morning I read in the *New York Times* that in the United States there are 55 divorces for every 100 marriages. Do they mean weddings? In any case, very frequent divorce is surviving a media shift toward endorsing imperfect marriages. Fears of AIDS aren't stopping divorce either.

Whether divorcing persons are technically "giving part away" or not, they believe they are. Splitting assets can be one of life's most pain-giving shocks. Practically speaking, preparation is key. Needed documents include bank, mutual fund, brokerage and other account statements. Tax returns for two years should be available. Collect any life insurance, real estate and loan papers. Details in writing about retirement plans, pensions and deferred compensation will be required.

You must for your and your lawyer's sake complete a cash-flow statement on your personal finances. A balance sheet (assets and liabilities) is also necessary. Use forms in this book for thoroughness.

Short term the standard of living even of millionaires takes a tumble during the divorce. Be prepared. Sort out your aims. Independence? Maintenance? Relocation? Rule out vengeance. It will just slow thing up and cost more.

Try to use mediation instead of the traditional adversarial method. One professional works with both spouses. Damages (financial, mental and moral) are much lower. If you find yourself in an acidic brutalizing end game designed to leave no survivors, give up. Get on with your remaining years. One of the multitude of screwed-up features of the divorce court system is the power it gives the uncooperative. Peace, in divorce, beats justice.

An important asset, the residence, should probably go on the market if it's too much house for one person. This is commonplace counsel, of course, but it's tempting to resist at first. Another important asset is any share the divorce grants you in your spouse's qualified plan, such as a pension or 401(k). Actually getting this money requires a QDRO (qualified domestic relations order) from court, by the way.

Courts award alimony at best to only one-in-six spouses, I've read. Even that low rate is declining. Remember alimony, unlike child support, is deductible for the payer and taxable to the recipient. Theoretically there are thus advantages here for a high-bracket payer and a low-bracket payee.

One of the too-frequent foul-ups stemming from divorce is "shared liability" as seen by the IRS. Say one spouse neglects to pay capital gains in selling a house share. The liability can go to the other spouse – I have a case now – if "single filing status" was not used at tax time. File singly if divorced or separated by court order. An option which works too is "married filing separately" status.

Again, let me say strongly from experience not to let matters drag on. There are many people who want to get even, who have power needs, who are on cash economies, who have money abroad, who know law, or who control finances professionally. Make the best deal with the opposing attorneys as soon as possible and hit the road. Time is fleeting, and you should be too.

*　*　*

Short answer: Make generous gifts to benefit others and your family. Use professionals. If divorcing, focus on cutting losses.

Chapter Seven

How to Pass It On to Others

In Chapter Four we were sizing up pros and cons of conventional estate planning. The question then was do we even want to maximize what we pass on to others. In the sense of what we are now talking about, inheritance or estate planning has two parts. One is how we structure finances for favorable performance and tax treatment. Presently we come to the other part, the part that should concern *everyone*. This is the orderly, convenient and considerate arrangement-making that one generation does for the next.

Inheritance Planning

Most millionaires have never led chaotic, irresponsible lives. We do the right thing wherever possible. In the case of planning for control to pass to others, the more we do now, the more control we have, and the more those left behind avoid depending on the doubtful comforts of strangers.

Wills

Some of you don't have wills. I think it's only about one person in four who does. Although we know Congress monkeys with estate law on an ongoing basis, many of those who have wills are still out of step with up-to-date planning philosophy. Will making remains the great example of approach-avoidance behavior.

What's wrong with dying intestate? Without a will, that is. Simply that the state, perhaps the least inspired and equipped organization conceivable, does your will for you. Is this terrifying enough? Assets frozen, court actions taking years, useless endless paperwork, guardians appointed. The worst thing is that people would often be appalled at how the government distributes assets when if finally gets to that. They apply fixed formulas.

Those of you who have wills must update them to reflect family changes. Marriage, divorce, children, grandchildren, death. You may have moved to a state where plans need to be modified. Your income and wealth levels have probably changed. All kinds of special circumstances, such as a relative with mental or physical limitations, may have developed.

Get this done professionally. Wills don't cost much, partly because lawyers may hope this is the beginning of a good relationship. As a prime example of why not to do it yourself consider Warren Burger, who as chief justice was the country's highest legal figure. Writing his own will on a computer, he fouled it up four-or-five ways. First, according to a Virginia estate specialist, his presumed taxes of $400,000 to $500,000 could probably have been avoided on his $1.8 million estate. Next, Mr. Burger made no provisions for sale of real estate or waiver of bonding, thus involving more expense and delay. Under Virginia law, the will wasn't self-proving, according to press accounts. As a result, witnesses would have to come in and testify and so on. If he seems somewhat clueless, what chance do we have? Hire a lawyer. Remember, too, wills are often challenged.

What does a will do? It deals with assets held in our own name. There are other assets – insurance payoffs, trust money, IRAs, jointly held things – that go to heirs irrespective of wills.

So, make a list of assets that will not pass directly to others when you die. They must go through probate. Name a guardian yourself for your children. Name an executor to handle the estate and a trustee for any trust.

Letter of Instructions

If you die unexpectedly, a letter of instructions is an informal service you provide for your loved ones, friends or associates. It lists your accounts, professional relationships with associates, lawyers, brokers, trust officers, doctors, and so forth. Specify exactly where your important documents may be found. Wills, powers of attorney, titles, birth certificates, policies. A copy of the papers should be kept by someone who doesn't live at your place. Avoid safe-deposit boxes in this case because banks seal them at death.

Remind whoever reads the letter to notify your boss to activate benefits. Update your list of assets and include it in the letter. Some elementary words of investment wisdom can be a relief to anyone overcome with sudden feelings of excess responsibility. It's always good advice to go slow. And include a note about particular funeral or memorial plans that you desire, if you like.

You get the idea when you put yourself in others' positions. One last helpful paragraph could cover emergencies you foresee. Who'll the kids stay with? Where are all the keys? Who handles services around the house, and when?

Probate

Probate by dictionary definition is the official proving of a will as authentic. If the deceased left a valid will, there is someone to be officially appointed to administer the estate. Probate Court oversees everything.

Assets must be collected, estate property must be protected and debts and taxes must be paid. Finally, once determinations as to who's entitled to what are made, property is duly distributed to new owners, the inheritors.

Although taxes are based on the net estate, probate costs are usually a percentage of the gross estate. An example is a house with a large mortgage. No matter. Probate charges calculate on the value of the house regardless of mortgage. It's a capital idea to get the fee question settled before legal work intensifies. Whether your state sets statutory fees or, like mine, "reasonable" limits, count on a single-figure percentage. Massachusetts probate costs, for example, run between 3 percent and 7 percent of gross estate value. You might inquire of your lawyer if his firm would bill by the hour instead of by percentage.

Time delays and contesting of the will can spoil the progress of probate. Although most work on the process usually winds up in nine months, when taxes are due, final settlement often takes two years or more. However, my sister, a teacher, used her summer vacation to administer and wrap up my father's good-sized estate with minimal assistance. I think the problem with probate is the unexpected.

Trusts

This is a good place to reacquaint ourselves with trusts. Why? Because there is one simple trust that lets us skip probate. It's called a living trust, but there seem to be a dozen different ways to say it. I'm talking about the revocable kind.

Like a will, the living trust document contains your instructions on how to manage and distribute assets if you die. Also, and here it's hugely superior to a will, it tells what to do if you're disabled. Wills can't do that, so people can go through the nightmare (it's too mild a term) of competency hearings, living probate, conservatorship and guardianship.

Although you change the owner of the assets from you to the trust, essentially you continue running your life as before. That, incidentally, is the secret. Because a trust owns the assets now and when you're dead, ownership doesn't have to be "proved" as in probate.

Unlike a will, there are no effective challenges to a living trust. Also unlike a will, this type of trust remains private. Your assets aren't dumped on a table in the town square, as it were, for the nosy to inspect. Probate, on the other hand, bares all.

It costs money, though not a lot, to have a living trust set up. But guess what? There are no probate expenses.

Two more important facts: The trust can be canceled,

"revoked" at anytime with no adverse effect. Other trusts can't. Regrettably, there are no tax savings of any kind with a revocable living trust. Don't forget that you may use a professional trustee at any time.

Probably the next most common trusts are credit shelter and marital trusts or "A-B" trusts. This technique allows full use by each spouse of the $600,000 exclusion from gift and estate taxes. When a spouse dies, his or her "unified credit" of $600,000 is in effect usable by the survivor although the property's ultimate destination elsewhere has been specified. Done correctly this bypass arrangement shelters up to $1.2 million from estate tax.

If you're in the middle of a circumstance where these types of trusts were established, an aggressive gifting program by the survivor can be considered. By loading up the $10,000 per person "freebie" gift, a surprising amount of money can be transferred easily over a few years. At least you're moving the total to be taxed somewhat closer to the $600,000 remaining. Use kids, grandchildren, in-laws and the like as recipients. It's legal.

Things usually to avoid include giving via forgivable loans, giving via powers of attorney and having someone other than the grantor gift out of a revocable "living" trust. The IRS can see any of these as red flags. Forgivable loans must be carefully documented and "real," with interest. Highly specific powers of attorney to make a gift are needed for this to work. Some states don't even permit power-of-attorney gifting under any circumstances. It's possible tax law changes will come that allow someone other than a revocable trust grantor to gift. Right now it's too dicey: If made before three years pass from the grantor's death, the gifts become part of the grantor's estate.

Generation-skipping trust (GST) applies to a method that doesn't seem to work as well as it once did. Your children need to be so well off they don't need an inheritance. Actually they can get some income from a GST. Taxes in a GST prove tough. The trust itself is included in the originator's estate. He or she, the grantor, could have been hit with a gift tax. And if the trust exceeds $1 million, there's a special generation-skipping tax. Hallelujah. It's 55 percent. Be very careful when transferring family business estates. They quickly exceed $1 million in many instances.

QTIP (qualified terminable interest property) trusts allow income to a surviving spouse during his or her lifetime. When the survivor dies, the remaining assets pass as indicated in the will of the first spouse to die. This trust helps when there have been multiple marriages, say, or when a business owner wants to guide ultimate control of the business. Couples who keep their own money separate find this most useful. When the survivor dies, however, the QTIP trust's entire value comes under the estate tax cleaver.

Unlike other countries, we tax the estates of all citizens and people who just live here.

Non-U.S. citizen spouses face a potential disaster with estate taxes. As you know, husbands and wives, since 1981, can leave each other, or give each other, an unlimited amount tax free. Tax law writers soon saw that a non-citizen could dodge all estate taxes by then taking assets out of the United States.

Seven years later a new law limited the amount citizens can leave non-citizens tax-free to $600,000. Congress simultaneously created the Q-Dot or Qualified Domestic Trust (QDT). You won't need a Q-Dot if assets in question don't exceed $600,000. Splitting $1.2 million solves a non-citizen problem, as does the obtaining of U.S. citizenship before or within nine months of the spouse's demise.

If the non-citizen is a resident (a holder of the former green card), he or she can receive $100,000 a year as gifts without encroaching in the citizen spouse's $600,000 lifetime gift and estate credit. For non-residents, by the way, that $600,000 becomes only $60,000. Note that I said non-residents, not non-citizens.

Q-Dot doesn't shine all that brightly. It's your only hope, though, to fend off estate taxes on everything above the one-person unified credit amount. The Q-Dot defers taxes until the death of the second spouse or until principal is distributed. In other words the first estate isn't closed.

Trustees must be citizens or American companies.

Sticking with specialized needs, a Minor's Trust receives donations that are controlled by a trustee who, to avoid tax liability, should not be the same as the grantor. This trust, also called a Section 2503(c), can last till the beneficiary is 21 or beyond. Uniformed Gifts to Minors accounts, by contrast, become property of the minor at 18 in many jurisdictions.

A minor's trust may cost $2,000 more or less to establish. And income is taxed at trust rates. Growth investments thus prove wisest. The idea is that whoever can contribute up to $10,000 a year should throw it into the pot. Why? Children who are young now may spend hundreds of thousands to get a degree.

Irrevocable Life Insurance Trust (ILITs) let us accomplish a couple of important things. If ownership is separated from the beneficiary, policies are not part of anyone's estate. If life insurance is paid to a named beneficiary, don't forget, it escapes income tax.

Also known as "wealth replacement trusts," ILITs, I understand, can be set up with "family banking" provisions, permitting the borrowing of money. As I say, I'm not a lawyer and personally have not seen this done. It could be a real tax advantage, if doable.

Should the value of the annual premium qualify for the gift tax exclusion, there's no gift tax. Along with avoiding estate tax, it avoids probate too. And the payoff is fast, compared to settling an estate.

Easy as pie, then? Not at all. Many people aren't insurable. Control over assets is surrendered. Drafting and accounting fees add up, as do any costs of professional trusteeship. In my experience go or no go depends on how the costs stack up vs. the benefits. There's usually no debate whether it's worth it or not at that point. Either it is or it isn't.

Staying with the question of transferring significant wealth, have you heard of the GRAT or GRUT? Or even the GRIT? These "grantor retained annuities trusts," "unitrusts" or "income trusts" permit wealthy parents to gift to heirs. A byproduct will be lower estate taxes for the benefactors. The grantor keeps income for a term of years. Then the beneficiary receives the principal.

With grantor-retained trusts, you position assets outside the estate. The grantor's income interest, whatever that happens to be worth, reduces gift taxes if you use up your $600,000 exclusion.

GRAT or GRUT? Typically you use the GRAT for yourself for 10 years. Then convert the instrument to a GRUT for the heirs. GRAT payments are level and may skim principal. The unitrust (GRUT) may bring rising income as an annual valuation affects the payout.

Testamentary trusts with some sort of trust organization as trustee come into being at the originator's death. Probate is the means through which this happens. I think their most common reason for existence is simply to have professionals running the financial assets you leave to children or maybe even a spouse. I'm told that somehow a testamentary trust may bypass the estate of a life beneficiary. See a lawyer if interested. I know even less about another supposed plus: Testamentary trust assets can be immune from certain government claims. Again, ask a legal specialist.

Charitable trusts of various kinds were covered in the last chapter (page XXX through XXX). The lead trusts and – more typically – the remainder trusts can deliver combinations of income tax advantages, capital-gains tax avoidance, and estate tax alleviation. As we discussed, one's income and inheritance amounts can be sustained and even enhanced in the face of serious charitable donations.

QPRT stands for Qualified Personal Residencc Trust. It gets your home out of your estate but lets you keep on living there. After a term of years, the ownership transfers to the continuing trust or beneficiaries. If you die before the term, however, the residence goes back in your estate. A key plus in QPRTs is that the value of the donated assets is frozen for estate tax purposes, even if market value ascends. And that value itself is reduced by the worth of the retained residential rights. You transfer property at quite a discounted value.

Medicaid or nursing home trusts avail themselves of whatever irrevocable legal means that may be found to buck nursing home bills to the taxpayer. At the millionaire level, all or most long-term-care costs could be met by income thrown off by the trust. It's patently ludicrous for millionaires to try to qualify for welfare anyway.

Your trust lawyer will remind you that jurisdictions won't wait forever to take a whack at the assets in a trust. South Dakota does not put a time limit on trusts. Your grandchildren and even great-grandchildren could thus benefit from a dynasty trust there. The big caveat persists that no one should put more than $1 million in any kind of trust that skips generations. But once you pay gift taxes to fund the trust, if just keeps on ticking. Family banking clauses can authorize withdrawals if needed or wanted, don't forget.

Incentive trusts come with all kinds of stipulations and restrictions. The grantor tries to control the beneficiaries' behavior. My personal view is that usually trust incentives testify to failed relationships. However, side effects of junk culture and social entropy never bypass the inheritors of wealth. There are certain types of parasitic acting out, in fact, that only the rich can afford to do. If you're considering an incentive trust, I'd run this by a psychological counselor first. It just may be that you're using the trust to achieve something that could be dealt with less indirectly.

Disclaimer trusts, which clients have asked me about occasionally, don't apply to us. Like nursing home trusts, they're for people who haven't seven-figure assets to protect. A disclaimer trust simply lets the living spouse inherit everything. That not enough assets exist for a credit shelter trust drives the creation of a disclaimer trust. The inheriting spouse has the right to disclaim a portion of the estate. In other words, you in effect inherit less for taxes' sake. Your children or alternative heirs receive the disclaimed assets via an earmarked trust.

There are so many disabled children we realize wherever the subject comes up. It's good that a special fund can be set up for a disabled child. It's called a Supplemental Needs Trust.

Sound complicated enough? Actually the world of irrevocable trusts beneath the surface teems with devices and interpretations far beyond anything a non-professional such as I could feature.

There is one last important trust, the living trust, that I must return to. Revocable at any time, this entity takes over and owns your assets. Everything else continues as before. There are no tax advantages of any kind. Because the trust owns your assets, however, there need be no probate. You still run the show.

Another huge advantage of living, or inter vivos trusts, is that, unlike wills, they can arrange for disability. Unlike wills, living trusts are hardly ever challenged. I've never heard of a single effective challenge. And they're private. No exposure to the public of the decedents' financial condition occurs, unlike probate.

Living trusts turn out to be much faster than probate for wrapping up an estate. I think this is a leading reason for growing consumer demand for living trusts. People who have waited for years to inherit their rightful share feel settlements delayed are settlements denied, at least partially.

Do I insist you'd be crazy not to obtain living trusts? No. The exception is that if you have a minor child. A living trust restricts the court's interference to simply approving the guardian. No overruling of your trustee choice is permitted. No fooling with the inheritance by the court is allowed. (I don't want to digress, but we have to remember that wills let courts control minor children's lives. Courts appoint guardians and control assets. Decisions and transactions require court approval. Full inheritance passes to the child at legal age.)

My guess in writing *What To Do With A Million Dollars* is that most readers no longer have minor children. If that's so, what counts most I think is a trusting and reciprocal relationship with a lawyer. In this relationship you discuss costs and timetables to the point where you're satisfied. Let the outcome of your decisions decide whether you go the trust or will route.

The living trust idea, still gaining adherents, heated up in the 1980s. It seemed that the next hot idea after the living trust was the charitable remainder trust. Now in full throat, the CRT needed a fair amount of space several pages back for me to get the concept across.

Family Limited Partnerships

The other technique now basking in financial planning fame is the family limited partnership. Not a trust, the FLP is supported by a simpler idea. The general partners, who run things, need not own more than a token portion of the partnership. Older and let's hope wiser family members can continue in charge while ceding meaningful ownership to heirs. The owners are called limited partners. Part of a cynical old adage is that general partners have the experience and limited partners have the money. It's not unusual for the general partners to hold no more than 1 percent of the partnership. The rest is given away to limited partners, who may well be children or grandchildren. The gifting of 90-something percent may happen all at once or slowly.

In the case of lawsuits, and remember I'm no lawyer, a limited partner's interest remains immune to creditors. If these assets include family business or real estate items, the attraction is clear. Homes are sometimes placed in FLPs, but every FLP should have a defensible valid business purpose. I must add that this last rule seems more honored in the breach at some of the hard-sell FLP seminars.

Besides the immunity from creditors advantage, FLPs benefit from minority stake status and impaired marketability. How? Well, an asset that you don't control ("limited" partner) and that is less easily salable deserves to be discounted, say 30 percent or so, for gift-tax purposes. The assets have to be transferred to the FLP, like a gift, for tax purposes. If they're discounted, more can be transferred cheaper. Warning: Assets discounted too aggressively may be subject to penalty taxes up to 40 percent.

The size of the discount depends on the assets involved and the terms of the partnership agreement. Proceed as if you're going to be audited, though there are advisers who recommend assertive discounting of 50 percent or more. Can you spell *red flag*?

One last matter. Partnership interests ordinarily go through probate. The case for using a revocable living trust, which avoids probate, to hold partnership interests isn't hard to build. And any advanced estate planning solution, such as a family foundation or limited partnership, should be part and parcel of an ongoing relationship with a law firm experienced in establishing and *maintaining* these entities.

Remember the Q-Dot trust? How it could benefit non-citizens? The need for us to follow special procedures for non-citizens stems from yet another nutty American tax peculiarity.

People who live in our country and who aren't citizens are called domiciliaries. The United States taxes our domiciliaries. Other countries don't tax theirs, I remember from State Department days. If you're not a permanent resident alien (card holder), you base your tax payments on a weird formula. If you hold a card, you pay the same taxes as a citizen.

One big lapse in the estate planning business recurs too often. Brokers, lawyers, accountants and trust officials routinely forget to establish where the client is a citizen. We may simply assume clients are U.S. citizens, sometimes with unhappy outcomes. See page 164.

Rules for Foreigners

However, what if I, or you, want to retire abroad? To become a domiciliary over there somewhere. Or just move our business and household. Any problems? You bet.

Once again the endearingly quirky American tax system strikes. U.S. citizens owe income tax to Washington on all income earned anywhere. It's a matter of faith with many expatriates that the Internal Revenue Service pays plenty of attention to them. Our government takes taxes from foreigners who live here, at the same time taxing us if we live there. Heads they win, tails you lose.

Suppose you run into foreign taxes on your income. Although every country is a special case, many places that are popular with Americans give credit for taxes paid here. And some places levy no local taxes.

It's not unusual for Americans successfully to classify borderline funds as capital. Abroad this can often serve as a shield against foreign income tax.

As to Medicare, it doesn't work except inside the United States. Millionaires shouldn't mind this, perhaps; but there are usually waiting periods of many months before free foreign health insurance, if they supply it where you are, takes effect.

Someone said that expatriation is the ultimate estate plan. In this sense expatriation assumes the surrender of U.S. citizenship, not just moving overseas. It's a free country. I think, though, that giving up your citizenship for money, even a lot of money, shows bad judgment. It places money ahead of other values. Nothing is valued that is easily obtained, goes the saying. Well, getting your citizenship back would not be easy for anyone. And it's common sense that if you need to protect a huge fortune, your residual holdings will always be far more than you will need anywhere. Even if you rationally experience our tax system as confiscatory.

Terminal Illness

Way over in the corner of our minds for most of our adult lives is the awareness that we could come down with a terminal disease. Not one, in the old joke, that you caught in a bus station. A chronic condition could shift into high gear and grow threatening.

Medicine, positive attitudes, prayer and who knows what increasingly bring us back from the brink. But that's no reason not to prepare for the worst. (This remains true for all planning, not just terminal illness.)

Needless to say, estate strategies or dying-poor plans should be in place as soon as they can. Read all your insurance fine print word for word. If you're working do the same with your benefits guide.

In extreme cases a good medical policy can pay off in six or even seven figures. Thus its value can't be overstated. After all, how much is your home worth, for example?

If you can increase your insurance at work – life, health or disability – simply by entitlement, you had probably better do it if seriously ill. Don't switch jobs at this point, except for extraordinary reasons.

Continue to fund tax-favored retirement vehicles. You may be in a lower bracket when disabled. Speaking of taxes they're a disadvantage if you use a viatical-settlement approach. That's when you sell your death benefit, remember, to a company now for a big discount and they take over the payments. When you die, they collect. Death benefits don't incur taxes but viatical settlements do. Wonderful.

No matter how well off you are financially, don't be surprised at the occasional liquidity problem when you're badly off physically. Make sure your portfolio provides plenty of cash-equivalency at this time. One stopgap to remember is credit cards to fight clogged-up insurance conditions. I haven't tried this but they tell me you can buy a credit-life plan when getting a card that will pay off charge card debt when you die. Check it out if interested. If you're like me you get two-or-three mailers a day for a "cheap" credit cards with big borrowing lines. I'm looking at an MBNA Platinum Plus brochure that came today for my wife. The credit line is "up to $100,000."

Funerals

At some point something has to be said about funerals. It's not exactly a finance question: Funerals I'm aware of don't approach superweddings for account-denting damage. This book isn't about last rites, and I'm not saving this section for the final pages.

After house, car, college and weddings, an ordinary funeral could be a household's largest expense. Let's count on at least $10,000. I don't see millionaires fussing too much over standard funeral pricing practices at the time we use professionals. Like policemen, morticians and funeral directors may not be perfect, but we're glad to pay them to do their job. My experiences have turned out quite positive. And I did read Jessica Mitford at a vulnerable age.

One refreshing course that lightens some of the sadness is donating organs. Tens of thousands of desperate Americans await various needed body parts. The entire body can go to a medical school for donation purposes and to be used to teach doctors. Some, perhaps most, medical schools make all this relatively easy. Though no one in my family has yet chosen this route, it appeals to both heart and mind, doesn't it?

Talk to Your Family

In all of advanced society we encounter the contradictory avoidance of discussion of crucial matters. Whether it's sex, money, death, depression, pain or illness our instinct too often is to skirt the issue. One major part of passing on to others your material worth, however, is open deliberation as to what's best overall for family and friends.

Durable Power of Attorney and Health-care Proxies

Absolutely essential documents must be made official. I'm talking about a durable power of attorney and some kind of health care proxy or living will or both.

Bear with me if you've heard all the horror stories around the country about conservatorship or living probate or about being declared *non compos mentis* (not of sound mind). Skip the following two paragraphs if this isn't new to you.

Living longer we are more likely to have our affairs taken over by a court than was the case. As with children, in my view, the very last thing on Earth to be allowed is for a court to "supervise" your affairs. Extreme slowness, even lethargy, is the rule. Remember jury duty? The O.J. trial? Many months pass by with little apparent result. Funds may eventually be freed for long-term care, but other equally important parts of personal asset management often take a back seat. Are the individual's needs and disabilities really considered when conservators are appointed? Not even in many, many instances. Is there sufficient monitoring of referees and others? Guess!

Is it expensive? What do you think? Is it awkward, public and potentially humiliating? And how! If you were to free-associate around people who've been through any of this, you, would hear "nightmare," "inaccessible," "ghastly," infuriating," etc.

We have covered one way out – the revocable living trust. Recall that, unlike a will, this unique trust deals with disability. The standard tool universally recommended is the durable power of attorney. *Durable* ,in short, means persisting through disability. Durable POAs, while not exactly required with a living trust, work well in combination.

There's no valid argument against executing a durable power of attorney. It lets someone pay the bills, collect money, cash checks, buy and sell securities, sell houses, open and close bank accounts and do other financial chores. The only sticking point is to whom to give the power. We were just referring to how critical it becomes to talk over major matters with one's family or friends. This is an outstanding example.

What has worked for me has been family meetings. Not only can we make clear all that is involved, we can start to divide responsibility. Meetings force us to think of income, including Social Security, real estate, insurance, brokerage and bank accounts. Standard durable powers encompass all these "issues." Writing in limitations of course is possible. And in some locales, your legal adviser may want to set up a "springing" POA. Disability activates springing powers.

If you do this yourself, and most people shouldn't, get your stationery store or document service form witnessed. Notarization is usually needed too. Ask your bank and broker if they require a special form.

Among the majority of families who should seek

legal assistance are those who practice gifting to reduce the future estate. The federal government's position now is that attorneys-in-fact (those with the POA) must have specific written authority to make gifts. I believe only Virginia among the states has specifically legislated a gifting right under a general power of attorney.

In your state, suffice it to say, your durable POA will probably have to state that the attorney-in-fact has the power to make gifts. Your lawyer may write "... make gifts in the pattern I have used ..." Specific types and sizes of gifts may be considered. Don't forget that spelling out details can prehandle potential family squabbles.

Let's segue from the financial to the durable medical POA. Although I haven't yet experienced this way of arranging for health crises myself, this type of power designates some carefully chosen someone to make care decisions. What we most use in Massachusetts and many more places is a *health care proxy*. I guess it's sort of the same thing, if you're incapacitated. The proxy is a person signified on a form.

These efforts to ease the indecision, guilt and powerlessness surrounding critical illness, accident or end-stage deterioration go by the generic term *medical directive*. A term I've encountered in New York is *health care declaration*.

An associated document called the living will is thought by the less informed to cover all these ill-health bases. But some places (New York, Michigan, and Massachusetts) don't recognize living wills. We need a proxy. But I recommend that Bay Staters who want one have a living will, too, in case something happens in a state where they do work. A living will declares clearly the type of treatment wanted if the afflicted can't make or communicate decisions.

It bothers me, though, that "living will," a very positive thing in a sense, has been transformed buzzword style into some sort of *ersatz* societal cure-all. Like "no-fault" divorce" or "zero-risk" standards, it sounds better than it is. The living will transfers power to the doctor, not to the family. No more informed consent, in other words. It can happen that treatment which would help someone isn't used.

This is a private decision. Again, I'm not a lawyer. It's just common sense, though, to explore as an alternative a durable power of attorney for health care or some similar alternative. Someone besides the doctor has say-so.

Disabled Children

The sensitive topic of disability also applies to children. I'm not thinking of children in the sense necessarily of young in years. The special poignancy of older offspring, perhaps middle-aged, who need more spent on them than the minimum arises often these days.

The trust called supplemental needs is an obvious help. Involving reliable persons from the disabled child's generation can add peace of mind. I'm hardly qualified to dissect this question. Lawyers, with your help, can establish a chain or web of responsibility. Just knowing that arrangements are in place to survive you fully rewards strenuous exertion on your part now.

Business Transition

Another vital family question to be resolved as far in advance as possible turns on the transition of a family business to new owners and/or management. The low numbers of businesses that succeed in staying in one family should depress anyone. Fewer than one in three family businesses endure into the second generation. For the third generation it's one in 10. The main hurdle of course is the tax law which requires cash payments when illiquid assets, such as businesses, investment real estate or farms, change hands. I read that the average life of a successful family business is 24 years.

Business owners chronically defer having their legal and financial advisers design a succession plan. But they desperately need to start answering three questions this minute. How will the government value the family company? Who will inherit the business? Who will manage the business should the present bosses die? Surprisingly a new common question is should the children's fiances sign prenuptial agreement's to prevent dissolving the business in a divorce.

Essentially no one knows the value of a non-public company. The IRS will say high (more taxes) and you'll say low (less taxes). Fortunately estate taxes can be deferred if closely held business interests top 35 percent of an adjusted gross estate. You can pay interest-only for five years. The rest of the money due can then be retired in 10 equal annual payments. A lifesaver.

You may have heard also of the Section 303 redemption. Again, if the business exceeds 35 percent of the estate, the business may buy stock back from the estate without creating tax impact. The amount shouldn't total in excess of estate taxes, administration and funeral costs.

Why not just give the business away? The taxes are too high, generally. "Estate freezes "have become legal again, with new complications. Don't listen to Tom Neely on estate freezes. Listen to your lawyer. What you want to achieve is the gifting of value today that will hence prove appreciable.

Several persistent estate planning problems are solved by buy-sell agreements. Writing this type of contract demands specific legal skills. Buy-sell agreements provide ready markets for business shares at the owner's death. Remember, though, not all estates will prefer to sell. Buy-sell agreements fix share prices and, we hope, estate tax values. Unwanted new shareholders cannot go around a good buy-sell agreement and bring disruption.

Special Problems

As the century winds up, the meaning of *family* has expanded faster than laws and contracts. Many safety-net features remain that protect and assist spouses, for example. But what of unmarried couples?

When a husband or wife dies without a will the survivor still stands first in line to inherit. That's not the case if there's no legal marriage. Committed unmarried couples must thus do wills pronto. Each should ideally use his or her own lawyer. The reason for this is to deny the conflict-of-interest argument to someone challenging the will if only the survivor's lawyer was used by both parties.

Challenges in my not-too-broad experience tend to occur during probate. How do we finesse this? Property, such as real estate or financial assets, may be listed as held jointly with the right of survivorship. Giving away more than $10,000 a year could trigger gift taxes, remember. An *unmarried* partner has only a $600,000 gift or estate tax lifetime exclusion. For married couples there's no limit. Don't add the partner's name to the deed without knowing the implications.

One straightforward way to provide for someone is to make the partner the beneficiary of bank accounts, life-insurance contracts, benefit plans or IRA's. You could also try it with brokerage accounts.

Let's not forget that revocable living trusts avoid challenges. What they require is near-absolute confidence in the trustee. The other signal advantage not to overlook is that avoiding probate lowers costs much of the time. Vastly less waiting will be needed after a person's death before red tape concludes.

This is as suitable a place as any to remind committed unmarried couples to arrange for durable powers of attorney with each other as attorney-in-fact. At the same time give each other legal authority on health care decisions.

As gay couples know only too well, in the absence of all kinds of contracts and authorizations and designations of preference, the relationship is almost presumed not even to exist in a meaningful way. Abandoned spouses have recourse in court, of course. But in case of a breakup between unmarrieds, everything about ownership of assets, how they were acquired and how they would be divided, should be in writing. At least make a joint videotape so you'll have something to use for backing up a claim.

I wish I knew more about the latest twists in unmarried and/or same-sex unions, but let me leave you with a motivating thought. If your lawyers and you haven't put together a structure of protection, you will likely see the partner's family assume power and ownership, even to disposition of remains.

Two lawyers who wrote a book called *The Living Together Kit* emphasize that just creating a contract is a helpful step. They also talk about what to do before you have children, if that's a possibility. And they note which states still outlaw cohabitation.

Speaking of cohabitation, have you heard of cohabitation agreements? When one cohabitant's money far outbalances the other's, a terminated living-together relationship might turn up in court. If "palimony" is sought, I'm told a cohabitation agreement becomes your strongest defense. Every detail of a relationship can serve as fodder for stipulation in the documents.

If asked to sign a cohabitation agreement, run it by at least one lawyer. And ask yourself hard questions about the wisdom of persisting in a relationship of questionable trust and quality.

Even more serious than cohabitation agreements are *prenups*. Growing increasingly standard at high executive levels, prenuptial agreements can even play a part in how welcome someone is to a new executive suite. The lack of a prenup in a non-perfect marriage could cool off venture capitalists or bankers.

All legal trends end in excess, perhaps. Prenups show no sign of ending, but the excess is already there. So-called equitable distribution these days can treat a professional practice as a jointly created asset. Then prenups matter. Wealthy successful women now must think of what will happen if divorce threatens. Prenups now exist that curtail spouses' career options or that put in writing an already warped balance of responsibilities. Almost everything can be *agreed* to. Courts will have to sort out just what one can actually be *held* to.

A few weeks ago I was listening to Dr. Laura while driving home. A lawyer called in about how he had delayed his wedding ceremony to add an amendment to the prenuptial agreement. This California couple had stipulated who purchases the groceries and who cooks which meals, and so on. Call me quaint, but the whole point of marriage is not me first. Rather, marriage itself can dissolve the prison of self. Think hard before placing more stress on avoiding the negative in a relationship than endorsing the trust.

* * *

Short answer: Bring as much order as you can to taxes, transition and death. Left unstructured, the money elements of life's last third meet a treacherous welcome.

Afterword

Don't Let Money Dominate Your Life

We know what Coco Chanel felt when she drew the line between those who "have money" and those who "are rich." The rich are handed their own set of difficulties about how to tell which people are trustworthy. Which people warm just to great wealth itself? They use those who have it. *C'est tout.*

The news ceaselessly pours out word of security problems and other special anxieties afflicting the contemporary rich. I think least among the problems of the truly rich may be those kinds of things the previous chapters hash over: The particular means of getting what we want and need from the money that we have.

The problem facing those of us who "have money" is not to let it assume too much importance. Another quote: "Money is like a sixth sense without which you cannot make complete use of the other five." Somerset Maugham. I take this to mean only that money facilitates living. You can work your senses without becoming a sensualist.

Let's call up a health-and-fitness analogy. Being healthy and fit facilitates living. But becoming too concerned with it is pathetic. The same kind of thin membrane that separates even the most financially conservative from ruin separates the well from the ill. And there's only so much you can do about it. Plutus, the Greek god of wealth, wasn't a hypochondriac. But it's common to find millionaires obsessed with not losing their money. A good exercise I recommend to combat this psychogenic crepe hanging is to visualize yourself poor. Think how you'd live. Think just how you would squeak by on low income.

To most people's surprise this exercise doesn't depress. If anything, it liberates. Living in black and white is still living. Non-essential materialism falls away. Then, if you've diligently put your financial affairs aright, switch back to Technicolor.

Just as healthy personal habits after a while really are habits, not efforts, financial grace grows with practice. Thinking and spending "net" and not "gross" becomes second nature. Rather than see one's own financial caretaking as an endless chore, we can take heart. The maturity factor mentioned prominently in the Introduction comes into effect. First you provide for all the matters you can control. The investing. The charities. The insurance. The inheritance stuff. Then you rest.

It's like building a cabin in the woods. You build it as well as you can. Once you accept that you can do little to stop tornadoes, forest fires, plundering grizzlies, rising taxes, you stop yourself from worrying about it. From worrying about what you can't control. Much as we'd like to dream otherwise, the woods don't care.

A practical piece of advice is not to let business, investing and financial so-called news sway you. We're going through a boom in disconnected data. Eventually, and readers may not survive to witness it, some way of filtering, clarifying and organizing this data overload will be found. Right now it's up to you to stay even without being overly concerned. Don't worry. Your friends and advisers will prove only too happy to alert you to this week's scare. A month or two later, of course, it will be forgotten, having been followed by other crises, also to be forgotten.

A client of mine who was born in 1955 remembers when knowing how to get information put you ahead of the game. He believes his contemporaries are the last group for whom this was true. Now, he points out, it's knowing how to sift out just what you need and no more that gives you an edge.

I hope this modest effort did not add to your overload. Knowing some of what's inside will give you three-quarters of what you can learn to preserve your capital. I admire do-it-yourselfers in some cases, but don't fear to use good professionals freely. Keeping up with everything steals too much irrevocable time in its flight. Trust, and don't forget to verify.

Appendix A

Withdrawal Duration

Payout Rate	6%	7%	8%	9%	10%	11%	12%	13%	14%	15%
10%	5.3	17.2	20.2	25.7						
11%	13.2	14.5	16.3	19.1	24.1					
12%	11.6	12.6	13.8	15.5	18.0	22.7				
13%	10.4	11.1	12.0	13.2	14.7	17.2	21.5			
14%	9.4	10.0	10.7	11.5	12.6	14.1	16.3	20.4		
15%	8.6	9.1	9.6	10.2	11.1	12.1	13.5	15.6	19.5	
16%	7.9	8.2	8.7	9.2	9.9	10.7	11.7	13.2	15.0	18.7
17%	7.3	7.7	8.0	8.4	8.9	9.6	10.2	11.2	12.5	14.4
18%	6.8	7.1	7.4	7.7	8.2	8.7	9.2	9.9	10.8	12.1
19%	6.4	6.7	6.9	7.2	7.6	7.9	8.4	8.9	9.7	10.5
20%	6.0	6.2	6.4	6.7	7.0	7.3	7.7	8.2	8.7	9.3

Rate of Return

Percent Return on Investment

Given a certain payout rate and a certain rate of return on investment, the tables shows the years an investment will last. If return is greater than payout, money lasts indefinitely.

Appendix B

Personal cash flow statement

In the spaces under the headings for each month, enter the amounts for this year. If last year is more representative or complete, use it. You will be composing your personal cash-flow statement on the worksheet.

Income

	J	*F*	*M*	*A*	*M*	*J*	*J*	*A*	*S*	*O*	*N*	*D*	*Annual Income*
Salary													
Self-employed income													
Consulting fees													
Director fees													
Trustee fees													
Retainers													
Commissions													
Bonus													
Pensions													
Royalties													
Residuals													
Alimony													
Child support													
Inheritances													
Gifts													
Trusts distributions													
Dividends													
Interest													
Asset sales													

Social security													
Annuities													
Loans receivable													
Forgivable loans owed													
Other receipts													
Total income													

Think twice before wrapping up the income worksheet. Don't disregard the odd interest or dividend account. Make sure that any empty spaces are correctly so. Fracturing an income stream into little bits this way helps to weed out oversights.

Moving on to expenditures, detailed breakdowns are grouped into large categories, such as housing or insurance premiums.

Expenses

	J	*F*	*M*	*A*	*M*	*J*	*J*	*A*	*S*	*O*	*N*	*D*	*Annual expenses*
Regular monthly outgo													
Housing													
Rent													
Mortgage													
Property taxes													
Utilities													
Telephone													
Repairs/Improvements													
Homeowner's insurance													

Domestic help	_ _ _ _ _ _ _ _ _ _ _ _	________
Clothing	_ _ _ _ _ _ _ _ _ _ _ _	________
Food	_ _ _ _ _ _ _ _ _ _ _ _	________
Groceries	_ _ _ _ _ _ _ _ _ _ _ _	________
Entertainment (at home)	_ _ _ _ _ _ _ _ _ _ _ _	________
Lunch	_ _ _ _ _ _ _ _ _ _ _ _	________
Insurance premiums		
Life	_ _ _ _ _ _ _ _ _ _ _ _	________
Disability	_ _ _ _ _ _ _ _ _ _ _ _	________
Medical	_ _ _ _ _ _ _ _ _ _ _ _	________
Automobile	_ _ _ _ _ _ _ _ _ _ _ _	________
Property & liability	_ _ _ _ _ _ _ _ _ _ _ _	________
Valuables	_ _ _ _ _ _ _ _ _ _ _ _	________
Long-term care	_ _ _ _ _ _ _ _ _ _ _ _	________
Other	_ _ _ _ _ _ _ _ _ _ _ _	________
Transportation		
Automobile loans	_ _ _ _ _ _ _ _ _ _ _ _	________
Lease payments	_ _ _ _ _ _ _ _ _ _ _ _	________
Commuting expenses	_ _ _ _ _ _ _ _ _ _ _ _	________
Gasoline	_ _ _ _ _ _ _ _ _ _ _ _	________
Service	_ _ _ _ _ _ _ _ _ _ _ _	________
Repairs	_ _ _ _ _ _ _ _ _ _ _ _	________
Inspections	_ _ _ _ _ _ _ _ _ _ _ _	________
Tolls	_ _ _ _ _ _ _ _ _ _ _ _	________
Garage	_ _ _ _ _ _ _ _ _ _ _ _	________
Taxis	_ _ _ _ _ _ _ _ _ _ _ _	________
Other	_ _ _ _ _ _ _ _ _ _ _ _	________
Education		

Tuition	___________	________
Room & board	___________	________
Fees	___________	________
Books	___________	________
Medical	___________	________
Gifts		
Birthdays	___________	________
Holidays	___________	________
Anniversaries	___________	________
Other	___________	________
Contributions		
Church or synagogue	___________	________
Charities	___________	________
Political	___________	________
Alumni	___________	________
Entertainment		
Vacations	___________	________
Club dues	___________	________
Dining out	___________	________
Plays, sports, movies	___________	________
Hobbies	___________	________
Books, magazines	___________	________
Other	___________	________
Loans		
Margin	___________	________
Educational	___________	________
Other	___________	________

Taxes		
Federal income		
State & local income		
Property (other than home		
F.I.C.A. (Social Security)		
Other		
Investments		
Investments		
Payroll plans (e.g., 401K)		
Savings		
IRAs		
Alimony		
Child support		
Child care		
Dependent care		
Personal expenses		
Grooming		
Professional fees		
Petty cash		
Other		
Spending total		

Subtract the lesser of your expenses and income from the greater to get the "excess" or – dreadful thought – deficiency.

Appendix D

Trusts

Trust Name	*Tax Features Gift/Estate*	*Income*	*Non-tax Advantages*
Credit Shelter; Part B of A-B trust	Shelters $600,000 from from estate tax.	If distributed, taxed to beneficiary; balance to trust at trust rates.	Investments may be managed for family.
Marital trust; Part A of A-B trust	No estate tax at death of first spouse.	Taxed to spouse.	Will or living cre ates trust to benefit surviving spouse with income plus principal.
Generation-Skipping Trust	In grantor's estate, special tax if exceeds $1 million.	If accumulated, taxed to trust; if paid, taxed to beneficiary.	Asset management for grandchildren; income to children possible.
QTIP-Qualifying terminable interest marriage	Taxed in second spouse's estate.	Income to spouse; capital gains taxed to trust.	Keeps some assets from spouse, as in second or wealth disparity.
Qualified Domestic Trust (QDT)	Though tax deferred until second death, in grantor's. estate	Taxed to spouse; capital gains taxed to trust.	Professional management available for spouses on trust assets.

Trust Name	*Tax Features Gift/Estate*	*Income*	*Non-tax Advantages*
Minor's Trust [Section 2503(c)]	Not in grantor's estate if not trustee.	At trust rates.	Main use is saving for college.
ILIT – Irrevocable Life Insurance Trust	No estate tax; unless premium exceeds annual exclusion, no gift tax.	No income.	Replaces wealth donated to charity, helps with liquidity at death.
Grantor Retained Trusts	Not in estate; gift tax after discounting.	Taxable to grantor.	Grantor retains income for a term of years GRIT, GRAT, GRUT.
Testamentary Trust	In creator's estate, but no gift tax.	If distributed, taxed to beneficiary; otherwise to trust.	Provides for supervised management of funds for children and/or spouse via probate. Inalterable after death of creator.
Charitable Remainder Trust (CRT)	Avoids except non-spousal income interest.	Beneficiary taxed only on income. Current deduction and avoidance of tax to grantor.	Maintains income to grantor, avoids probate, permits diversification and benefits charity
Charitable Lead Trust (CLT)	Lower liability as income to charity cuts value.	None.	Preserves estate but benefits charity now.

Trust Name	*Tax Features Gift/Estate*	*Income*	*Non-tax Advantages*
Qualified Personal Residence (QPRT)	Retained residential rights cut value for gift tax. Asset value frozen		Inheritance, value of residence remains same as when trust created, despite margin gain. Grantor can stay in donated residence.
Dynasty Trust	Gift tax consequences. Generation-skipping tax if donation exceeds $1 million.	Taxed to beneficiary.	South Dakota lets trust last indefinitely. *Assets tax taxed at transfer only once.
Supplemental Needs Trust		Taxed to trust on amounts over $7,500.	Segregates funds for additional care of disabled child.
Living Trust	No implications for most families.	No implications.	Avoids probate, deals with disability. Less vulnerability to delays and challenges. Revocable.
Incentive Trust	Customized arrangements where payments to heirs hinge on compliance with trust terms. Trustees usually corporate.		
Medicaid Trust	Not for people with $1 million or more. Income produced would mostly cancel advantage.		

Index